FEB 2 3 2018

Confident
Digital Content

Confident Digital Content

Master the fundamentals of online video, design, writing and social media to supercharge your career

Adam Waters

KoganPage

Publisher's note

Every possible effort has been made to ensure that the information contained in this book is accurate at the time of going to press, and the publishers and authors cannot accept responsibility for any errors or omissions, however caused. No responsibility for loss or damage occasioned to any person acting, or refraining from action, as a result of the material in this publication can be accepted by the editor, the publisher or the author.

First published in Great Britain and the United States in 2018 by Kogan Page Limited

2nd Floor, 45 Gee Street	c/o Martin P Hill Consulting	4737/23 Ansari Road
London	122 W 27th St, 10th Floor	Daryaganj
EC1V 3RS	New York NY 10001	New Delhi 110002
United Kingdom	USA	India

© Adam Waters 2018

The right of Adam Waters to be identified as the author of this work has been asserted by him in accordance with the Copyright, Designs and Patents Act 1988.

ISBN   978 0 7494 8094 3
E-ISBN 978 0 7494 8095 0

British Library Cataloguing-in-Publication Data

A CIP record for this book is available from the British Library.

Typeset by Integra Software Services, Pondicherry
Print production managed by Jellyfish
Printed and bound in Great Britain by CPI Group (UK) Ltd, Croydon CR0 4YY

For Isla

By the time you're old enough to read this
the world will be very different.

CONTENTS

ACKNOWLEDGEMENTS

Firstly, a huge number of people helped me with this book and I'm grateful to all of them – my editor Anna Moss for answering all my daft questions, Meri Pentikäinen for introducing me to her, and to all my case studies who provide so much expertise and advice from so many different backgrounds.

I've been lucky in my life to have people who have given me a shot, believed in me and helped me grow as a person. So thank you to my mentors Jedge Pilbrow, John Davies, Steve Clark, John Holliday, Nicky Ness and Nick Pollard. Matt Muir, Jonathan Harper, Paul Vaughan and Luisa Bockmeulen all helped me find interesting people to speak to for this book. Richard Hutchinson gave me so much help with the radio section and I'm so thankful. He's someone who has dedicated much of his life to serving those who serve. Neil Hall helped with much valuable advice on photography – thank you, Shippers.

If I've forgotten to put your name down here, I really am sorry, but I suppose it's in print now so I'm stuck with the awkwardness.

Finally, thanks to my wife Anna and daughter Isla who are the lights of my life.

Introduction

A career in digital content means you'll get the opportunity to be creative, tell incredible stories and learn new things every day. It's fast moving, so you can always discover something new. You can communicate in lots of different ways – a video, an article or an animation. You can connect with people and champion the causes or organizations you feel passionate about.

The best part of it is that anyone can do this. You don't need specific qualifications, expensive equipment or exclusive contacts. All that's required is a desire to learn, creativity and a passion for telling stories.

What we mean by digital

Digital is a word that can mean many different things to different people. Organizations often use it to refer to technology such as cloud computing or app development. Digital media can mean streaming services like Netflix or computer storage. It can be confusing.

When it comes to digital content, I think of it as written, photographic, audio, designed or video content consumed mainly on a smartphone but possibly on a large-screen computer like a laptop. Thinking of it this way keeps things simple and clear. Social media has become an essential platform to share content on, but it could also be viewed through an app or mobile website, or shared through a messaging tool.

What this means for you

Because of the rapid and far-reaching rise of digital there is as a result an enormous demand for people with digital content skills.

The demand is also across virtually all industries and types of organization. This is very good news for someone who is interested in a career in digital content. Some people still have a hard time believing that producing digital content or understanding social media can be a proper job, but by building up your digital content skills you will hopefully find a lot of opportunities.

It's a competitive marketplace too, but for me, the best thing about specializing in digital content is the range of industries you can work in. If you are passionate about cooking you could work for a food brand, creating recipe videos and writing about baking techniques. If you are an outdoorsy person you could work at a national park, promoting the incredible views through an Instagram channel.

You may want to do something more serious, such as journalism, or even work in law enforcement helping promote the work a police force does. This list could go on and on, but hopefully you see that by specializing in digital content you not only get to be creative and have fun but potentially have a career that matches your personal interests too.

How did we get to where we are now?

It was just before the turn of the millennium that internet use became widespread, though still accessed almost entirely by desktop computers. With its rise, publishers (newspapers, TV stations, PR firms, anyone communicating with the public) quickly moved on to this exciting new platform, building websites to share the content they produced. Newspapers would create electronic versions of their daily papers, media companies would upload video clips to their sites, and radio stations streamed their shows. Still though, this early digital content would often just be the same as its real-world counterpart.

There were two major innovations that did the most to shape our modern digital world and its content: the rise of social media and the launch of the iPhone. The iPhone transformed the communications industry and kick-started the use of smartphones as we know it. Its ease of use made the internet accessible to everyone with a device they carried around with them. Quickly Apple's rivals moved to create equally impressive gadgets with powerful cameras and bigger screens. Social media allowed people to instantly and easily share updates, videos or images with a huge network of people. They could easily comment on stories and interact with public organizations.

Combining these two innovations – the smartphone with social networks – was revolutionary. People could broadcast to the world from wherever they were. The cameras on their phones were more powerful than kit that would cost vast sums of money only 10 years earlier. Smartphones would gradually begin to catch up on desktop computers as the main device people use to access the internet. You only need to look around the next time you're on a busy train for proof that more people stare at their phones than stare at a newspaper.

The rise of the smartphone forced publishers to reconsider how they share content with their audiences. What good is a widescreen video designed for a TV when someone is watching on their tall, narrow phone? A beautiful website designed for a large screen is impossible to read unless it can be quickly redesigned for a mobile screen.

The challenge of creating content that is compelling while viewed on a smartphone screen, through social media or a mobile website, has become its own format or speciality. Publishers quickly realized that digital content is unique. They began building specific teams to create video or written content designed just for digital platforms. TV channels would take existing footage and reformat it for mobile, making it more concise or vertical rather than widescreen.

Publishers who only existed on digital platforms soon sprang up. The most famous example is probably Buzzfeed, which now covers an enormous range of subjects and has a dedicated news team.

It's not just media organizations either. The free access to social media platforms and the widespread availability of smartphones means anyone can easily tell a story, provide information or market their products.

What this book is about

This book is designed to give you the fundamental skills you need to get started in digital content. I won't be going into details about specific social networks, and you won't find step-by-step guides to using specific apps like editing a video in Adobe Premiere. The principles are the important bit and don't change much over time. Once you understand how to produce a great video, you can look up a guide on using the app you choose. I want this book to be as helpful as possible, but an out-of-date guide to a program you don't use doesn't help anyone.

It will explain what good digital content is and how to make it. With this knowledge, you can then learn the specifics for the tools or networks you are using. With these skills you'll be ready to thrive in the world of digital content.

Before we begin...

The one thing I want you to keep in mind is: *you can do this*. Sadly, a lot of people I've met don't believe in themselves. They think producing a video or learning to write a compelling story is something they could never do. This is nonsense. You may be curious about digital content but have never done anything creative before. That doesn't mean you can't *now*. It is so important to have faith in yourself, keep optimistic and learn new things.

Each chapter of the book has a case study with someone who has worked with digital content either by accident or by design. It's a broad mix of people and I hope it will help show you why digital content matters to a lot of different organizations. There are also practical exercises at the end of each chapter. I encourage you to do them as it will allow you to put what you've learnt to the test and also leave you with a portfolio of work to impress potential employers.

Why digital content skills are essential for your career

01

- All organizations need great digital people.
- It doesn't matter what career you want – digital skills will help you.
- Digital content isn't just about communications.

Digital content is essential to any sort of organization. In this chapter you'll see that by learning these skills you'll be giving your career a real boost, and we'll also look at the fundamentals of why digital content skills matter.

Digital platforms have two important functions – they are sources of information and they let people communicate. Understanding how people share and respond to this information is essential to succeeding at digital content.

You may already be a diehard user of social media. You may even have built a large following because you're passionate about a particular subject. But have you run digital accounts for a major organization?

You may be able to produce incredible video. But have you shared those skills with others?

You may be an experienced digital community manager. But have you built a team with people who are nervous about digital?

You may be an experienced teacher of digital skills. But have you convinced sceptical bosses to invest in digital for your organization?

In this situation your passion for the networks you use or the stories you tell will help to achieve success. It's crucial you combine that knowledge and advocacy with an understanding of how the organizations you want to work for can use it strategically.

What if you have never used a social network? You may think there's no way you could produce a video or tell a story, let alone publish it to millions of people.

What has digital changed?

Major news stories are frequently broken directly on social media. With the popularity of smartphones around the world people can share information instantly from wherever they are. Events such as the Arab Spring or presidential elections have played out simultaneously in the 'real world' and on social media. Information, images, videos and opinion can be shared instantly. Smartphones, with their powerful cameras, allow people in the right place and at the right time to become instant citizen journalists. Newsrooms around the world have teams of reporters who solely monitor social media for breaking news stories, trending themes and powerful imagery.

A few years ago a helicopter crashed in London. At the time I was working as a journalist in a TV newsroom. As with any breaking story, we rushed a reporter and camera crew to the scene. It took them a long time to travel, to get an understanding of what was going on, to prepare for a live broadcast and afterwards to come back to the office. At the same time, my team was monitoring social media for the photos and videos people posted as the event happened. We sought permission and got them on air instantly, without having to leave the office ourselves (and while our own camera crew were still travelling). If you want to develop strong digital journalism skills, understanding the tools and techniques available to tell stories quickly and clearly on digital platforms will allow you to thrive.

More government services, such as registering to vote or paying tax, are handled online, with social media support teams on hand to answer questions. This is a strong example of how any major organization, commercial or public, needs to adapt for the digital age. While you might not work in the public sector, you could work for a large complex organization that provides vital services.

Government bureaucracy often (with good reason) has a reputation for being opaque and complicated. Anyone who has had to fill out a tax return will tell you that lengthy forms, slow response times and a lack of user feedback are common complaints. Important information and announcements are frequently just sent out as a traditional press release that few people see. Thankfully, many governments around the world are realizing the potential of digital. Not only does it make citizens' lives easier; it helps governments save money and become more efficient. Many have set up dedicated digital departments such as the United States Digital Service or the UK's Government Digital Service. Government communications teams have invested in digital training for their staff and stressed the importance of evaluation. Often, policy will be informed by digital research and data. So learning how to speak to citizens, hear their views and convey what government is working on in an engaging way is essential. As public sector communicators learn to produce clear, engaging content, they can make sure citizens are aware of important announcements and messages.

Perhaps the biggest impact of all has been on advertising and marketing. The popularity of smartphones and social networks combined with incredibly accurate data and analytics has made advertising more accurate and effective than ever before. Let's say you wanted to show an advert to every oenophile in Haslemere for your new luxury wine delivery service. In the past, you could put an advert in the local newspaper perhaps, or put leaflets through people's doors. How would you know how effective it had been? You might see a rise in sales, but was it because of those leaflets? Even before setting up your business, how would you find out how many wine fanatics there were in the area? How could you stop your leaflet deliverer from wasting their time by delivering only to wine lovers?

With digital advertising, you could show adverts only to people in the area who like buying wine and have enough disposable income to sign up to your delivery service, and you pay only when they visit your website. The fun doesn't stop there – you could capture demographic data about your customers and use those to improve your service. Perhaps you thought people from Haslemere would love claret. Instead you discover that Pinot Noir's all the rage and that people tend to order it on a Monday night. You could then start sending them vouchers for Pinot Noir every Monday and make a compelling video about the best foods to serve with the wine.

Digital content has also transformed charities – sometimes by accident. Amyotrophic lateral sclerosis (ALS) was, until recently, a poorly understood disease. That was until Pete Frates, a Boston College student diagnosed with it, started pouring cold water over himself to fundraise for charities researching the disease. It became a viral trend as the Ice Bucket Challenge. World leaders, celebrities, sports stars and perhaps your friends and family began dumping buckets of water over themselves in social media videos and challenging others to do the same.

In a month, $115 million dollars was raised. Great digital content allows charities to spread their message, share the good work they are doing and build an audience of dedicated supporters, while keeping costs low.

And what if you want to be your own boss and set up your own business? Digital gives you a fantastic opportunity to promote your service or product in an accurate and cheap way. By understanding how to make great content you can get your customers to do your advertising for you as they share your posts and watch your videos. You could create compelling stories and campaigns that help you raise funds to launch your business. The case study for this chapter shows exactly how useful digital content can be to an entrepreneur.

These are simplistic examples, but they show you the breadth and power of digital communications. Hopefully, by now common sense will tell you that virtually all organizations therefore need people with great digital content skills. You may want to go into business, work for a charity, become a journalist or even help run a country. Very different industries – yes. But all need to be effective at communicating digitally, with great content as the best way of doing so.

Everyone's digital now

It used to be the case that most organizations would never have to speak directly to the public. They might hire an ad agency to produce a flashy TV advert for them occasionally, or have someone send out a press release now and again. Since social media became so popular, all organizations are now publishers as well. It's quite rare for organizations not to be on social media. Naturally, they therefore need to put out great content on these channels. Skills that many organizations would previously just have outsourced are now a vital part of their workforce – content production, storytelling, editorial judgement, community building, advertising and so on. Without good content, organizations are wasting their time on social media.

Therefore, by gaining an understanding of how to produce digital content you are giving yourself a massive boost to how employable you are. It also means you can easily switch industries if you ever wanted to. Sick and tired of the big bank you work for? Find a charity looking for a social media manager, or set up your own business and promote it online. Your skills will still apply. So not only does learning about digital content boost your career prospects, it also gives you flexibility and security.

Often when I speak about digital content skills, someone will put their hand up at the end and say: 'But I work as an accountant/HR professional/office manager/etc. Why do I need to know any of this?'

Of course, there are roles that have no need for any sort of content production skills. But it's very rare indeed to find a role that has no need for at least an understanding of digital. Let's take those examples I just listed.

So you're an accountant. I agree, it's unlikely you'll be required to actually produce a video or manage a live social media Q&A with a senior member of staff. But by knowing how cheap and easy it is to produce great video in-house means you can stop the organization getting ripped off by unscrupulous production companies. Running a social media group for people in similar roles will not only raise your profile in the industry but provide an endless source of advice and support. What if you ever want to set up your own firm? It's likely you'd need to promote it yourself on social media and know how to use these tools to respond to customer enquiries or advertise your business. When there's a change in the tax code, there will be plenty of people searching online for answers about how it affects them. Wouldn't it be great if they found your explainer video first?

What use does an HR professional have for digital content skills? As I've explained previously, these skills are highly sought after. One of the questions I'm most frequently asked is: 'What does good digital content look like?' By being able to identify candidates with strong digital content skills you can ensure you get the right people into the organization. You can help the teams within the organization identify which roles would need digital content skills as well as adapting your training or personal development programme. Hachette Careers use digital to host online Q&A sessions, produce interesting visual content and answer questions candidates may have on Twitter.

It's essential for leaders or managers of any kind to understand effective digital content. This is something I explain in more detail in Chapter 8. For now, understand that digital content is your organization's 'conversation' with the public and other businesses. It's the words, videos and images that current or potential customers associate with your organization. Knowing how to commission great material, or how long it should take to make, at what cost, is a powerful skill to have. And as I've demonstrated, digital skills are in huge demand. As a leader, it's your responsibility to attract this talent. You're also there to make sure your digital professionals have the right autonomy, equipment and support to thrive.

A lot of effective digital content is about taking risk. It's about trying new things to see what works well with the audience. Your organization may be a very risk-averse one that has never done anything like a live video broadcast on social media before. But in a fast-moving world, where people have access to all the great content they could ever want, it's vital you experiment with what does and doesn't work for your audience.

It may fall on you to create this creative culture. Influencing others is a hard skill to learn, especially when you're trying to convince people much more senior than you. Being able to do so and demonstrate your success is a crucial part of any career you choose to follow – digital or not. Thankfully, with digital analytics it's possible to demonstrate in cold, hard numbers how well a piece of content has performed. Again, this sort of success is an enormous boost to your employability. The best leaders want people who will challenge them and push their organization in the right direction.

The digital skills gap

In the UK, the Science and Technology Committee has warned that the country is facing what it calls a 'digital skills gap'. According to the committee, 12.6 million adults lack basic digital skills.[1] While smartphones, social media and app distribution have all exploded in popularity over the past decade, something strange has happened – many have felt left behind or don't realize how these tools can improve their lives.

Anecdotally, in my experience many people (of all ages) are nervous about digital communications. I've dealt with plenty of cynical journalists or government ministers who disparage digital as something silly, or just for young people. I've also found that behind much of this negativity is fear. People worry they would never be able to understand how social media works and be seen as old-fashioned. Nothing could be further from the truth.

If you're a manager, the same principle applies – your staff may not want to admit that they feel this way. Assurance and understanding that there is a large digital skills deficit and putting the right training in place to deal with it will create an effective and loyal team.

Plenty of people have heard horror stories about social media posts going badly viral. The strength of social media networks is that information can be shared so quickly; naturally, this means content that goes down badly with the audience can be shared to millions within a very short space of time.

Despite working in this industry for many years, I have never lost that slight pang of fear as you press 'Publish' on a post to an audience of millions. But the best defence against posts going viral in ways you don't intend is by understanding your audience and building up your content skills. You'll quickly develop editorial judgement. Is this content right for the audience? Could it be misinterpreted? Is the timing of it insensitive? This is a subject I cover in more depth in Chapter 5.

A dangerous mistake many make is thinking of digital content as less important than traditional press releases, TV interviews or radio adverts. Even more deadly is thinking that digital communications is just a form of IT. I can't begin to count how many times I've been asked to fix people's computers. There was a time when e-mailing or using a word processor was seen as dangerously geeky. Now, being unable to use these tools would be incredibly unusual. So digital content and digital communications are really just another way of publishing or broadcasting, and soon I expect the word 'digital' will stop being used at all.

A couple of times a year I give a talk to military leaders about the future of the media and the world of digital communications. Here is a room full of people who have made life and death decisions, have led soldiers into battle and are responsible for the well-being of thousands of people. Nevertheless, some of them have quietly confessed to me that digital and social media makes them very nervous. If you feel nervous about lacking digital skills, you can rest assured that some battle-hardened generals do too.

It's crucial to understand that many people do feel this way. If you are looking for a job where you will use your digital content skills, you will experience this cynicism or nervousness. Taking the time to convert cynics and share skills that you may think of as basic is the only way to succeed if you're trying to make an organization more digital. It can be hard when something so obvious to you is disparaged or ignored by others, but, as with everything, perseverance is how you'll succeed.

Demonstrating you can change an organization's culture is another highly sought-after skill and one you'll often use working in digital communications. Business transformation is a complex subject and not the focus of this book, but, nevertheless, here are some suggestions for things you can do to build up digital skills within an organization. They certainly apply if you're building a business – you can keep them in mind as you grow.

Identify who your digital ambassadors are

When you start in a new role or at a new organization you'll quickly discover which people have talent or potential for making digital content. It may be a gifted video producer who hasn't been given a chance to publish their content on social media. It may be someone in the finance team who is a digital fanatic outside of work, or someone who is a natural writer. These people will become your most powerful assets when you want to build up the wider organization's digital content skills and understanding. You could be as charismatic as Clark Gable but it won't solve all your problems; people need to hear the message from others.

Identify who these people are, create a casual working group, and figure out how you can get everyone in your organization understanding great digital content. Remember, as everyone is now a potential producer with their smartphones, you can get them all on the lookout for great opportunities or stories about what the organization is doing.

You are also creating a network of digital supporters who can 'report back' on how things are developing in the rest of the organization. This will help you keep track of people's progression and how much different teams are learning. You can also discover who the cynics are, or those who are blocking others from being more digital.

Host regular digital events

Don't worry, I'm not suggesting you break out the smoke machine and motivational music. As I said before, many people are nervous about being creative and publishing their content. It's essential you create a culture of learning and experimentation so everyone can discover what effective digital content can do for the whole organization. Candid lessons about what has worked (and what hasn't) are powerful ways to get everyone understanding what good digital content looks like. Colleagues can also share tips with one another. Occasionally I've had to promise free pizza to make sure plenty of people turn up, but it always seems to work.

It raises your profile within the organization, too, and gives you a great example of showing initiative. If you're looking for work, you could run free events in your local area to offer advice to businesses and organizations. Plenty of people need help with digital and, who knows, it could lead to a job offer.

'Thought leader' is one of those business jargon phrases I dislike, but establishing yourself as someone who can share expertise on digital content is another way to boost your prospects. It will give you the chance to network and raise your profile in other organizations and industries.

Sharing the success

One of the most powerful aspects of digital communications is that virtually anything is measurable. If you put an advert in the newspaper, you won't know how effective it's been. Sure, you may know the paper's distribution numbers, or there's a special offer on the ad so you know which customers came from the newspaper. But other than that, it's extremely tricky to measure anything else. With digital you can measure how many times a piece of content has been viewed, by whom, for how long, on what device and at what time of day. These are just a few examples, too – the data you can capture are extremely broad.

These data give you a fantastic opportunity to demonstrate not only the success of digital content but also your own work. Few people are lucky enough to have such tangible information to prove how well they are doing. If you've started making more effective digital content and traffic to your organization's website has shot up – shout about it. Naturally this is a double-edged sword, as your failures will be measurable too. Relax about that though; digital content strategy is all about figuring out what works and what doesn't.

People unsurprisingly love to have their hard work recognized and rewarded. So use data to share the success. Perhaps it's a weekly company-wide e-mail showing what the top ten pieces of content are (and who produced them). You could host regular sessions to discuss what worked – and what didn't. You could even have a trophy for the top producers of digital content in the organization. If it's just you running your own business, then prepare to receive a lot of trophies.

By sharing the success, you create a positive culture that helps convert digital cynics in the organization.

The digital skills gap is good news for those who do develop digital skills, but a nightmare for employers. Deloitte's 2015 *Ascent of Digital* report states that 'changing an organization's workforce and skills is seen as the most challenging area to manage overall, and changing culture is particularly hard'.

All organizations need to recruit digital-savvy staff and retain the talented ones they already have. Perhaps this is the single clearest signal that by learning digital skills you can improve the chances of having the career you want.

The benefits of being multi-skilled

For the past few decades, in the media it was standard for even the simplest shoot to have a dedicated reporter, producer, videographer, sound engineer and assistant. The footage would then be sent to a video editor sitting in a large, dark, dedicated edit suite. One of the reasons for this was that the equipment needed to film, edit, or record sound was a lot more expensive. It was also less user friendly so required a lot of experience to use.

This is also one of the reasons why most organizations never had to think about producing their own content. They would just work with a production company (at great cost) who could produce the video or design work.

Organizations often wouldn't have their own distribution networks either. Can you imagine a government department or charity having their own TV channel? So not only did organizations lack the means or knowledge to produce content themselves, but they also had to pay to have it distributed.

The rise of digital media has democratized communications in two crucial ways:

- Cheaper, more powerful and more user-friendly equipment means anyone can produce content.
- Social media and websites provide free distribution networks for content.

As I write this, I can picture all the professional videographers I've worked with groaning. 'How can amateurs compare to the stuff we shoot on proper equipment?' It's true that people with these specialized skills will be able to produce very high-end material, and there will always be a place for that. But now, they aren't the only ones who can produce video.

Once cameras became cheap enough and laptops powerful enough, it soon became the norm for people producing content to shoot, edit, and have graphic design skills. When I started out, my specialities were producing and editing video. I soon realized, though, that employers needed people who could shoot video as well as having some basic graphic design skills.

Let's not be naive; by having multi-skilled staff, companies don't have to employ as many people or invest in as much equipment. This means that competition for these multi-skilled roles will be fiercer. There is a positive, though: more smaller organizations will be hiring content producers as the costs are lower.

The mentality that some people have of 'this is my job, I'll resist it changing, and my skills will always be useful' is unhelpful and obstructive. Everything changes over time, especially the fast-moving world of digital. Surely, if you're passionate about something, it's exciting to learn new and different things about it? I'll never forget the thrill of setting up my first shoot for an interview. I had to act calm while the interviewee waited for me to set up the lights, microphone and so on. Certainly nerve-racking, but fantastic once I'd finished.

Having a flexible, agile way of thinking is essential for all aspects of digital. Things simply move too quickly for a status quo to develop, and by embracing change you are setting yourself up to succeed. It can be hard when something you enjoy doing is taken away and your role changes. But you can't stay in your comfort zone (as tempting as it is).

By being multi-skilled you are not only making yourself more employable. By continuing to develop your skills you will also be more secure in your current organization. Redundancies are always dreadful, but sadly they are something most people experience at some point in their careers. Usually, the first people to go are those with expensive, very specialized skills that aren't needed any more. By remaining eager to learn new skills and by being multi-skilled you are reducing the risk of this happening. It's always good to plan for success, but reducing the risks of things going badly is important too.

How do you know which skills to develop, though? Let's say you're a graphic designer. Do you learn how to shoot video or photography? Animation or video editing? Keeping an eye on what social networks are asking for is a good indicator. When I first started managing pages on Facebook, the network was encouraging publishers to post simple, powerful images. I promptly brushed up on my photography skills and learnt some easy graphic design techniques. Facebook then announced it would start hosting videos directly and would promote them in people's newsfeeds. Being able to quickly pivot back to video production was invaluable. In 2016, Mark Zuckerberg, the founder of Facebook, launched a new live streaming feature and invited everybody, not just brands, to use it. Live video has some important differences, so again I looked at what skills my team and I would need.

Two other factors to consider when you're planning what skills to develop are what your organization needs and what your organization is good at.

Let's say you work for a bank. Your job is to keep customers aware of the latest security advice for their bank accounts. You're not marketing to them; it's important factual information. How can you convey this clearly and compellingly?

You could film video or take photos to share this information. But the bank you work in is a boring-looking place and you're only able to film in the office – not very visual at all. You do, however, have really clear, simple guidelines for people to follow. Therefore you may decide to learn animation so you can easily produce content at your desk without having to worry about how to show this security advice visually on video.

Let's contrast this with a luxury car company. The vehicles the company produces look and sound incredible, and it's easy for you to get access to them. Photography would be important, but you'd miss out on the sound and movement of the cars. Animation would be wasting the strengths of your brand – there's no chance to show off the cars themselves.

A frequent mistake many people and organizations make is trying to do everything at once. If, as an organization or an individual, you excel at producing great visual imagery, then don't spend time building up your writing and storytelling skills unless you really need to. There's only so much time, energy and resources you can call upon, so spend them wisely.

It may be odd in a business book to speak about having fun, but for me that's one of the best things about being multi-skilled. Learning new skills, being creative and trying new ways of producing content are always incredibly exciting. It may take time to learn new things, it may be far out of your comfort zone or from what you consider as part of your role, but the delight of discovering new things and the opportunities that arise from them is incredible.

Hopefully this shows you that by building up a range of digital skills, you not only make yourself more employable; you can have a lot of fun while you're doing it.

CASE STUDY Bunster's Hot Sauce

I spent a few years working alongside Renae, an Australian TV producer, churning out video news packages. One day, she came into the office announcing she was going to make her own hot sauce. Since then she's launched Bunster's Fresh, her own company in Perth, which has become a fantastic success.

She's featured on national TV, her sauces have gone viral on social media (partially due to their extremely rude names, unprintable here) and she's built a successful business.

The hot sauce market is a crowded one. When Renae started out, it was just her running the business with her own money as investment. She immediately started using social media to build up her brand and raise investment for expansion. I had a conversation with her about how creating a tone of voice and producing video content helped her build her business.

I got obsessed with hot sauces after a holiday in Mexico, so when I got home I made a batch of sauce. I thought it was rubbish so I gave it to my friends. They loved it and started demanding more of it (and started paying me). I believe this is what you call a 'business'. It's just got more professional and serious since then – that was in 2012. My business started with me cooking up 35-litre batches of sauce in my kitchen by myself. Once a photo of my sauce went viral I couldn't keep up with that demand, so we had to go to a factory. Now we cook 20 tonnes of sauce in a few days. So I used to make a few hundred bottles and now I make about a hundred thousand in a few days. And I don't have to inhale chilli fumes anymore.

When the picture of my hot sauce first went viral at Christmas 2014, there was an immediate correlation in sales spiking. It has always been that way. I can actually tell that a photo is going viral somewhere based on the sales that I see when I wake up. I'll wake up and see 50 sales, all from America and they all started after 1.30 am – I can tell a picture is doing the rounds in the United States. It's quite fun. At Christmas we can just put up a piece of good content, promote it and make it go viral because everyone is in such a gift-buying frenzy.

As the business started by accident and was really a bit of a joke to start with, the voice of the brand grew from there. Just generally being crass, rude and immature is my personality, so it was quite easy to just keep doing what I do and translate it into a brand. I didn't realize it, but the authenticity of my immature jokes really resonated with a lot of similarly minded people who (rightly so) hadn't yet found a brand that spoke to their love of rude gags.

The one thing I'd do differently? I wish I'd gone as crazy as I am now, right back in the beginning. Being wishy-washy and trying to appeal to everyone doesn't work. You have to pick your audience, speak to them and make them your tribe.

I have a long background working in many varied positions in TV. So when Facebook launched high-tech video capabilities, this was when I really found my feet on social media.

Video (and TV) is traditionally how stories have been told and products sold. Now, with a mobile phone and a bit of editing know-how you can be creating your own ads and putting them straight out there to your tribe. But I don't believe in constantly trying to sell to people. They switch off. Through constant funny (immature) posts I keep in contact with my audience and find like-minded people who will also hopefully like my products and decide to buy them one day.

I think it's easy to make any old video, but hard to make a good one people actually want to watch. It depends how much you want to succeed. You need to watch some tutorials on how to edit, and watch videos that you like the look of and use their editing techniques. If you don't know how to do it, watch some more tutorials. Pay attention to durations and how long it takes to get into the video. Most people click away after five seconds. So there are lots of things you need to learn to make a good video, but there are lots of hints and tips online. Or you can go and work in TV in London for ten years, like I did.

At the moment for my business, social media is great for finding customers and getting information off them so that I can expand into more traditional methods of selling my products. These include getting distributors and into retail outlets, which is where most of the face-to-face selling of my sauce goes on.

But what can't social media do for me? It can't convey the brand's energy and passion the way myself and my friends do at events and festivals. Someone could see 20 of my best social media posts and love them, but it would never compare to meeting a bunch of fun, happy people, who give you free hot sauce and corn chips and talk about how great the sauce is. It's really rare to get service like that in this day and age (of socially stunted people staring at their phones). So people will always remember that face-to-face meeting with me and my brand way more than some video of a guy snorting chilli powder and then coughing up a lung.

Becoming more employable

In the previous section I explained the benefits of being a multi-skilled digital content producer. But how do you go about actually learning these skills? Obviously, the downside of needing to learn a wide range means probably needing a range of training options too.

By buying this book you're certainly on the right track. But where do you turn for practical advice?

Thankfully, there is a passionate community out there you can learn from. There are plenty of options available to you, many of which are free. Let's look at some of the options out there.

Practical methods

Rather than spending the money on a course, you may decide simply to buy the kit you need instead and figure it out yourself. You could buy a DSLR (digital single lens reflex) camera and learn how to shoot both video and photography. Combine that with a copy of Creative Suite and a powerful computer, and you've got all you need to produce digital content. Whether this approach will work for you depends on how you like to learn. It could be easy to spend a lot of money on the wrong type of equipment, or get frustrated, without proper guidance.

This method means you are able to start producing content immediately, which, for most, is the fastest way to learn. I taught myself how to shoot and edit video by borrowing cameras from my university and using their one editing computer. It took a long time to figure out, and undoubtedly if I'd had some proper tuition I could have learnt much faster. On the other hand, though, I was producing content straight away without having to spend any money.

Some organizations offer a halfway option between a formal course and a job. A lot of publishers offer internships or work experience programmes. These have plenty of positives and negatives.

You'll be learning at a professional organization that produces digital content for real. It could be a news organization, a digital magazine or a creative agency. You'll get to spend time with professionals and find out how the industry really works.

There are drawbacks, though. Competition for these opportunities is fierce and they often rely on who you know rather than formal application processes. Too many organizations take advantage of enthusiastic interns by not paying them while asking them to work long hours. Make sure you're clear with the organization what you expect from the opportunity and make sure they stick to it. If the opportunity isn't paid, then the tough reality is you may have to work two jobs.

It can often be worth approaching organizations you'd like to work for or that you think you can learn a lot from. You may have to hound them, but you can create your own opportunity this way. Be utterly relentless. It can be tempting to try your luck at a huge famous brand that everyone knows. If you do manage to swing some experience there, that's undoubtedly a great opportunity for you. These opportunities can be few and far between, though. I suggest thinking carefully about what organization could teach you the skills you need. It may be dull or not in the industry you want to break into, but if you can learn the content skills you need it will give you a great chance to develop.

Even half an hour spent with a professional producer will be more valuable than a day's course in a classroom, so try to engineer whatever opportunities you can.

If you want to learn particular software packages for, say, graphic design or animation, most of the companies that produce the software have excellent guide books. These are usually cheap and are very comprehensive. They can be a good solution if you want structured guidance but have a limited budget.

Free methods

People who run training companies will hate me for saying this, but there is a fantastic free resource out there that will teach you anything you need to know to a very high standard. Once you've read this book you will know what you want to learn more about. Use it as a blueprint that you can refer back to when checking how your learning is going.

YouTube is an incredible place to learn new skills. For my house-warming BBQ I told everyone I was going to cook pulled pork, despite the fact I've never made it before or used a charcoal BBQ. By searching YouTube for tutorial videos on setting up my BBQ, cooking the meal and making sides, I ensured my party was a success. The same applies for content production. If you want to learn the fundamentals of making video, or editing, or a primer on graphic design, it's the place to look. In later chapters I will share some techniques for creating content, and by combining this with videos and practice yourself, you will learn much more quickly.

For any subject you'll be able to find passionate, helpful people who have created series of tutorial videos for you to follow. What's more, they are often very quick to respond to any questions you have. The quality of these videos is usually very high and they cover the basics of content production to very advanced concepts. Want to learn how to set up a video camera or animate special effects on to your footage? There will be a video tutorial for it.

Playlists are a really helpful feature of the site. You can create your own learning playlist and work through it at your own pace. People often share their own, too, allowing you to complete your own virtual course.

I don't just want to promote YouTube, though. There are plenty of active forums, social media groups and web guides on the subjects you want to learn about. They are filled with helpful experts, so don't be afraid to ask for guidance and support.

There are some drawbacks to learning in this way. A lot of employers may not see it as a proper method of learning, despite the quality of many of these tutorials and the time you dedicate to learning. It's a good idea to compile a portfolio of the content you've produced, allowing you to show your skills regardless of how you've learnt them.

And nothing compares to practical experience, be it from a professional or you finding your own way with the equipment and software. As mentioned before, many places are willing to offer work experience opportunities or let you shadow their professionals.

Many of the big digital companies such as Google or Facebook offer their own free online training courses. These are comprehensive and often recognized by employers. The drawback of these is that they are, unsurprisingly, designed to promote the company's own platforms. So while Facebook's advertising training is very good, it only trains you to use Facebook's advertising tools. You may have to do a range of these online courses to make sure you're not just taught to use one platform.

Demonstrating your skills

Using some of the methods above, you may have created a personal learning plan and spent the time to develop the skills you want. How can you then demonstrate these skills to potential employers?

To state the obvious, the great thing about digital content is it's a tangible, visual product that you can show off. It is crucial to create a professional portfolio of the content you've made to show the range of your skills. There are a number of easy options available to you.

Video showreel

Once you've made a few videos, it's a good idea to put a showreel together. You can host these for free on a video-sharing website, which gives you an easy way to show off your skills. Keep it concise and consider using graphics to add more detail. These don't necessarily need to be the title of the production, but rather facts and information about how you produced the piece.

Online portfolio

A number of really smart websites have launched that allow designers and illustrators to show off their work. Behance is a good example that again is free to use. If you're a photographer, Flickr is a very well-known service that also has an active community.

Interactive page

Websites designed to be online CVs have become popular. If you have a range of things you want to show off, consider using a website like about.me. You can link to all your online portfolios and give potential employers or clients one place to find out all the information they need.

Exercise

We've covered a lot of ground in this chapter, but two main themes stand out – identify which digital content skills you need to learn/build, and establish the best way of learning or sharing them. It's easy to try to do too much, especially if you're enthusiastic about digital. It may be you're in a job you dislike and want to switch to a career in digital content. How do you make the best use of the small amount of free time you have?

It's important to have a strategy and a plan in place for your personal development. This is especially important when you want to become a multi-skilled professional. This exercise is designed to help you get started.

For this exercise we will create a learning plan based on the skills you want to learn more about.

You may decide to specialize in one area of digital content. We've discussed the importance of being multi-skilled, but it could be video or graphic design you're specifically passionate about. If this is the case, I've provided specialist areas underneath each main subject in case you want or need to learn more about it.

If you can build up a moderate amount of knowledge for each subject, you will thrive in a digital content role. By following this plan, you'll make content that you can use for a portfolio when applying for jobs. This will allow you to demonstrate your abilities and make you stand out from the crowd when applying for a role.

Work your way through the list of skills, identify which ones you need, choose a learning method and then set yourself the outcomes you want to achieve. It's a simple exercise but one that helps you focus and gives you a plan to follow. I've suggested a few ideas on how to learn each set of skills, but do whatever works best for you.

Table 1.1   Digital content learning plan

Skill	Learning method	Outcome
Video Filming Editing Animation Live video	Borrow/purchase camera equipment. Watch online tutorial videos. Speak to an experienced producer.	Create a short video and show it to online communities for feedback.
Imagery Graphic design Photography Illustration	Analyse and replicate photos and designs you like. Shadow a photographer. Use free trials of design software. Try a professional day course.	Tell a story with photos or create an infographic about a subject of your choice.
Writing Storytelling Writing in plain English Proofreading	Read writing style guides. Write a short article about a subject you're passionate about. Try explaining a complex subject to a general audience.	Write a compelling piece with a catchy headline and offer it to publishers.

(continued)

Table 1.1 (Continued)

Skill	Learning method	Outcome
Social media Understanding the different networks Marketing Campaign planning Community building Editorial judgement Crisis communications	Study successful brand strategies. Create an advertising campaign for a fictitious product. Create a crisis response plan.	Create a social media group based on your hobbies or a subject you're passionate about.

Summary

Hopefully, after reading this chapter you now understand how you can give your career a boost by building up a range of digital skills. By doing so, you are an appealing hire for a range of organizations and industries. It will also make you more secure in the long term as your skills apply to many different roles.

You can develop these skills in a number of different ways that fit your available time and budget. It's important to be clear about what skills you do want to develop and create a learning plan.

If you are a leader or manager, it's important to think about creating a digital culture and work on making your organization more digitally focused. As a result, you'll be a more effective leader and again more employable.

In the next chapter we will begin looking at how to actually make digital content, starting with the most important skill – how to write.

Note

1 House of Commons Science and Technology Committee, 'The Digital Skills Crisis', June 2016

How to write for digital

02

- Plain English and a clear message are essential.
- Think about branding and tone of voice.
- Practise long-form writing.

It's easy, when speaking about digital, to concentrate on exciting new products or popular new social networks. Too often people talk about digital in terms of the future. What's coming next? How many people are using a particular service? How will the world change?

In a world of augmented reality and instant communication, it's easy to forget the fundamental skill all digital communicators should have – writing well.

When digital platforms started becoming popular, many predicted this meant a shift to information becoming short, to the point, succinct, shallow even. Twitter's 140-character messages seemed to signal a wider trend: that people wanted incredibly short updates on their phones and social media feeds. Who in a busy world would want to read full articles or stories on their phones?

Publishers started creating new formats to try to appeal to busy distracted people. 'Listicles', usually credited to Buzzfeed, became a much copied style. You can spot them easily:

Seven Things This Book Will Teach You About Digital Content

Here Are Five Reasons Why Confident Digital Content is the Greatest Book Ever Written

The Amazing Photos That Reveal the Secrets of Incredible Digital Content

These articles are usually photo-heavy lists with a headline designed to tease people into tapping and reading more. These sorts of head-line are called clickbait.

The explainer is also a popular format, especially with news organizations. People often crave simple explanations of complex news stories. It can be a useful technique for marketers too – proactively answering the most common questions from customers means they don't have to ask them in the first place.

Something unexpected happened alongside the popularity of these short, disposable styles – the rise of digital long-form writing. Audiences also wanted to read complex, informative articles and stories. A report by the Pew Research Centre from 2016 showed that people spent twice as long actively reading in-depth articles on their phones as short-form articles. If they weren't interested in long reads, they would simply have left the article.

Websites and apps that feature long pieces have flourished – The Atavist, Longform or Longreads, for example. New writing tools that allow anyone to create beautiful articles are also extremely popular – Medium being the most famous.

So we find ourselves in a world where two kinds of written content are most popular:

- very short succinct updates that catch people's attention or explain something complex in a simple way;
- in-depth, engaging storytelling that people want to spend time reading and discussing.

Clear, engaging language is at the heart of both styles of writing. However, they do require different skills. Over this chapter we will look at both short-form and long-form writing and how you can improve your skills with both.

This chapter will provide general advice rather than specific style or grammatical suggestions. There are many incredibly good style guides out there.

It's important to remember that the way you or your organization uses language is just as important to your brand as visual guidelines.

By improving your writing skills you will be supporting your career, no matter what role you want to pursue. You may not end up writing lengthy pieces of creative genius. But the ability to explain complex issues in compelling, clear English is such a powerful skill to have.

Short-form writing

'Men walk on moon' – a famous newspaper headline that manages to tell the whole story in four short words.

Thanks to the popularity of smartphones, most people now have access to unlimited amounts of content and information. Today, writing compelling headlines is just as important to the digital producer as it is to the tabloid headline writer.

Social media is often used by organizations to point audiences to their products or websites. If you use social media, have a look on your newsfeeds. Which posts catch your eye? What is it about how they are written that means you want to find out more?

As you will see, eye-catching headlines and short, interesting sentences are an important tool for gaining people's attention. People often complain about short attention spans; if it were true that people in today's world can't focus, Netflix would be out of business. There's a reason why people binge-watch hours of video on it – it's high-quality storytelling that people want to watch at a time of their choosing.

It is true, however, that people quickly scroll past content on their social media feeds. They don't take in much of the information in an article or form. Often, when you're using digital platforms to speak to people you will be trying to convince them your content is important. It could be an in-depth new report, a video you've worked hard on or a new service that may help them. You will have only milliseconds to capture their attention with just a few words. No wonder people obsess over each individual word. You're hopefully now seeing why being able to write in a clear and compelling way is so vital.

But the importance of clear writing doesn't end there; once the audience visits your website, article or report, you must make sure they quickly get what they went there for. Many websites have complicated language, lengthy unnecessary introductions and unclear guidance, which means frustrated users.

Writing a great headline

Accuracy and clarity should always be your values when writing. Many organizations use social media to deceive or provoke people.

Being clear and accurate doesn't mean being boring, and you will often need to write an exciting headline. If you're making a big announcement, have an important story or are launching a new product, you're going to need to shout about it with a great headline.

While there is no exact science explaining what makes a great headline, we do know what one is designed to achieve:

- Summarize the story, product or idea in a few words.
- Entice the reader into finding out more.

You can achieve these goals in a number of different ways. Think of most social media posts as headlines – you want to be as clear and as interesting as possible.

Let's pretend, after too many sandwiches spilling out on to my shirt, I've decided to create an ingenious new product called edible sticky tape. You wrap it around your burger and *voilà* – no more ketchup on your shirt. Sells itself, right? Sadly not – I need to write some compelling social media posts to promote it. Before we look at effective headlines, let's look at what a bad post on social media would look like:

> Edible sticky tape is a new type of adhesive strip that is engineered to maintain the consistency of your meal choices. It will robustly contain all manner of liquids and food items. It is available to purchase from our e-commerce store that can be found by searching the internet for edible sticky tape. It can be used in a variety of ways but must be applied properly for full effectiveness. Purchase now if you're interested.

Ghastly. But why?

1 Far too lengthy. The human eye will skip over a dense block of text like this in a visual newsfeed.

2 It's full of complex, technical language.

3 It doesn't make edible sticky tape sound compelling or exciting.

4 It doesn't have a clear call to action or an easy process to find out more.

5 It does a very bad job of explaining what the sticky tape does.

You don't need to resort to tabloid headlines, but the same principles of brevity apply. It's also likely you won't be able to solve all of the above in one sentence. Still, clarifying a message into just a few words is crucial.

Let's look at some of the types of headline you could use:

- Alliteration – a technique that always helps a phrase stay in people's minds:
  - *Edible Sticky Tape – the secret solution to spilled sauce*
  - *Don't let dinner dates be disasters*
- The tease – entice the reader into finding out more by not giving away all the answers:
  - *Keep your shirt safe from stains with this crazy sticky tape*
  - *Can burritos and sticky tape work together?*
  - *This guy got tired of leaky burgers – so he invented a solution*
- Numbers – a very popular technique is using numbers to catch the reader's eye. Note how some of these don't actually mention the product and add an element of mystery:
  - *Five table manner tricks you've never heard of*
  - *Four ways to stop your kids causing chaos at dinner*
  - *Three incredible ways to pimp your burger*
- The shout – when all else fails reach for the metaphorical foghorn:
  - *Stop spilling and buy this!*

These are just suggestions. You will need to develop your own in-house style and it's crucial you retain quality. It can be tempting to go overboard, but this has become known as clickbait, which I discuss at the end of the chapter. You'll see in the exercise that taking products or complex announcements and creating punchy headlines for them is a useful skill to keep fresh.

Brevity

Something that's taught to many journalists and communications professionals is explaining complicated subjects as simply as possible.

A common challenge would be: 'Imagine I'm a caveman. Explain the internet to me.' It's surprisingly hard the more you think about it.

What this is designed to do is to avoid assumed knowledge. It's easy to assume what the reader will know. You may think something is incredibly obvious, but it's always safest to assume the reader doesn't know what you mean.

It's my belief that the basis of all good communications is explaining things simply and clearly. It takes practice and can be much harder than it looks.

When it comes to digital media in particular, we mustn't waste time. People want to get the information they need as quickly as possible. Every time you write, you must ask yourself: Is this as clear and as simple as it could be?

Every industry and profession has its own language and jargon. some engineers may understand what a complex maritime environment is. For the rest of us, it's probably just the sea.

Unless you're speaking to peers, you must not lapse into using this sort of language. It isn't understood by your audience and it confuses your message. Some of this jargon may be obvious – some less so. It's worth looking back over the content you've written in the past and see what language you've used that could be made clearer.

Great teachers are often described as those who can explain a complicated concept as simply as possible. When writing for digital, you will have to be like them. Write in a natural way that speaks as simply as possible to your audience. It's worth thinking about it from your perspective, too – when you look up information online or browse your newsfeeds, when have you found the information easy to understand? When is it unclear, and why?

The beauty of plain English

We all have friends who are grammar pedants. You know the type: taking joy in highlighting missing possessive apostrophes or arguing about the Oxford comma. Perhaps you're one of them.

Bad spelling and grammar get a lot of attention. Something that is often forgotten is the importance of plain English: clear, simple language with a name that makes it sound a bit boring. The previous section emphasized that using plain English is essential, but too many organizations use a pompous, complicated tone of voice:

> *Going forward, actionable analysis will be undertaken to better understand the requirements of our stakeholders to drive greater innovation within the professional sphere.*

No one likes to be spoken to in this way. Many professionals think that using this sort of language makes them sound more, well, professional. It's telling that none of the leaders people look up to speak or write like this. None of the famous plays, reports or speeches from history are written in complicated jargonese. Some people may also think that using big, fancy words make them sound clever. There's nothing smart about it.

Convincing others in your organization to accept that this is how your business should be communicated publicly can be a challenge. They may feel that you're not capturing the nuance of what the organization is doing or that the language isn't as accurate. There can be some truth in this, which is why it's impossible to be completely prescriptive about language.

Despite the importance of plain English, don't feel worried if you're not a confident writer. It's definitely possible to over-analyse everything you write and there will always be people who misunderstand what you're saying. Yes, it's important you think about writing clearly and review what you've written, but there's no need to agonize over everything you write. If it has a human tone of voice and it's clear what you're trying to say, then you've nailed it. Some people like to say 'write like you speak'. If you actually try doing this, you'll find a jumble of words, stops, starts, slang, tics and so on. There is an element of truth in this advice, though – by using more relaxed, natural language, your writing becomes easier to read.

Writing for websites

Unless your website is full of fascinating stories, people will skim-read it rather than reading everything fully. The people writing the content for your website may not like it, but the truth is that people will quickly skim over the information to find what they want.

To complicate things further, they won't read things in the same order, unlike a book going from left to right. So not only do you have to consider what you're actually saying, but also how you're presenting it. To make things even trickier, they will be looking at your website on an enormous range of devices, from large desktop computers to smartphones.

Thankfully, a lot of research has been done into how people read on websites. You can commission research that actually tracks people's eye movements while looking at your site. The field of user design and experience (often called 'UX') has also grown dramatically, with many people specializing in it as a career. Good UX means your website will look good on any device and be easy to use.

If you're going to design or write content for a website, there are some steps you should make sure you follow:

- *Create a style guide or tone-of-voice guide so that all the language has a consistent style.* A style guide can be as detailed or as simple as you like – it could be the size of a small novel or one page. To be successful it should have advice on which words to use and avoid, what jargon or misspellings are commonly used, and advice on how to respond to comments/questions from your audience. This guide will evolve over time, so it's good to have regular updates on what's changed.

- *If your budget allows, make sure you have an experienced UX designer as part of the project.* You may not have the funds to hire a UX designer, but they are extremely important so they should be a high priority. They will ensure the site is easily usable by the audience and can act as editorial quality control for the content on the site. It's easy to spend a lot of money on building websites, but if they don't work well, it's wasted.

- *Conduct user research to see what works with your audience and what doesn't.* How do you know if the content you have produced for your site works? It's very easy to assume, wrongly, that what the site says is clear. Once a website has been launched the work doesn't end – it's vital you then test it with your audience and see what needs to be improved.

- *Use analytics.* There are various tools that enable you to see what sections of the site are most popular, what people are searching for before finding your site, and what devices people are viewing your site on. You can then adjust the design of your site accordingly and see what can be improved.

If your site is one that has news stories or updates posted to it, make sure these are prominent. They are news stories for a reason and you want people on your site to find them quickly.

You should also include compelling, attractive images and graphics to break text up. They help lift an article or page and make things more interesting for your audience. It is possible to include audio too, but use this sparingly. Audio can be a very powerful tool for storytelling when combined with text, but it should be built into the page very thoughtfully. Use clear signals to stop and start playing, avoid anything playing automatically, and use audio only when it is really necessary. Many news organizations have experimented with including audio in their writing on digital platforms with great effect.

The visual design of your site improves the written content too. By using a clear, bold font people will find everything easier to read. It can be tempting to over-design, with lots of colours, styles and complex fonts. But this makes everything on the site harder to use and dilutes the message you're trying to get across.

By planning your website content carefully you will be more credible and effective with your audience. Improving the content on your site is an ongoing process, so remember to frequently study the analytics you have, conduct user research and look at how people actually use your site rather than how you think they do.

Long-form

As shown earlier in the chapter, long-form writing has enjoyed a renaissance on digital platforms. While great writing is not an easy skill to learn, it is a very effective method of communicating, especially because it doesn't need any expensive equipment or tools. If you have a powerful story to tell, it has the potential to reach millions.

Long-form pieces typically:

- are a few thousand words in length (although they can extend into tens of thousands);
- are usually non-fiction but not necessarily journalistic;
- are based around very high-quality writing;
- may include other forms of media or interactive site design.

You may want to consider a long-form piece if you have a subject that requires a lot of explanation, is emotive or is simply a great story. Long-form writing can still be used in a commercial way too. If you're launching a product or setting up a business, why not think about telling the story of what inspired you to do so?

There are risks with long-form writing, though:

- The need for high-quality writing means it takes practice to succeed.
- It is easy to drift into waffle when short, concise writing might have been better.
- The subject matter has to be interesting enough to maintain the reader's attention.
- The website or platform hosting the writing has to have a clean, uncluttered design to avoid distracting the user.

When planning a campaign or story, decide which elements of it are best suited to concise updates and which could suit long-form writing. If you're unsure, have a look at the websites mentioned in this section to get a feel for long-form writing. It's probably the hardest kind of digital content to do well, but there's nothing stopping you practising to build up your skills.

CASE STUDY   Christine Cawthorne at Crocstar

Christine runs a company called Crocstar that specializes in digital content – especially written content. She's built a career and a business around writing for digital platforms after starting out in journalism.

When I was five, I wrote a story called 'Frog and toad have a picnic'. It was an instant hit with my family and I declared I would be a writer for ever more.

2.1

I studied journalism at university because I was good at English and I thought it would be quite glamorous to be a reporter. Turns out it wasn't, but it did make me realize how much I loved telling stories.

My first job after university was managing the student newspaper. It was hard: long hours, managing the budget and making sure we were on the right side of the law. After a year I knew I wanted a more junior position so I could learn how to do things properly. There were internships at Yahoo, which at the time was one of the coolest new companies to work for, so I went for it. I got a position as an assistant content producer where I chose the news and content that went in the prime position on the homepage. It was the time of Britney videos and iPods so there really was something for everyone.

I must admit I got a bit obsessed with looking at what users clicked on. The idea that you could see whether what you'd written had been looked at – and clicked on – by people was incredible to me. I learnt so much about tone of voice, persuasion and short-form copy by writing headlines and teasers.

After that, I worked as an online journalist at the BBC for a few years. Excitingly, I once said 'Hi' to Adrian Chiles. Here I combined the art of telling a story with the competition of having your story on offer against lots of other interesting and original content. Obviously I always wanted my content to be that week's 'most read'.

Writing for digital is different because when you're online, you're in a particular frame of mind. You're motivated to find the answer to something. You've sought the answer out yourself, usually by starting a search query.

You know what it is you need, or want, to do.

This idea is so powerful that it changes the entire experience of reading. And it should also change the way that you write content. Think about how much that person already knows. How much context they now no longer need.

Typically people want much less copy online. They don't want to spend time reading – they want to understand something almost by absorbing it.

If you can learn about people's online behaviour by seeing what people usually do on the website then you can start to understand them better. Even if they're watching cat videos the whole time, you'll be able to see what else they do online. You can think about the whole journey that the person is going on – and what they're looking for during each stage. That helps you decide how to split up the information and where to put it.

With digital content, it's always housed in a particular design, and that's a constraint you may have to work to. The copy is being *used*: it's being clicked on, copied and pasted, moved around and hidden. It's way more active than if it's on printed material.

To be a digital writer you need to be confident in your language skills. You need to be able to distil complex ideas down to their component parts and you need to be able to explain those ideas using simple language.

You don't need to be a native speaker but you need to be able to understand things clearly. Then use your target audience's language in your copy so it feels familiar and natural for them.

Research shows that people with both low and high levels of literacy prefer to read plain language, so being comfortable using everyday words and simple sentence structures is a must. You don't need to be a full-on grammar nerd.

I also say that being a digital writer is not an ego trip. No one should notice your words – they should just be part of the overall user experience. You're not trying to get people to notice how clever you are as a writer (sorry). But you're helping people achieve their online tasks, which is its own reward (and sometimes you can sneak puns into copy – but you didn't hear that from me).

Apart from having excellent writing skills, you also need to be able to empathize. Sometimes you will be writing fun copy but there is a huge need for sensitive copy. You need to be able to imagine you are the person using the site or app and imagine what frame of mind they're in.

Related to that is having the confidence to be logical and human. As a copywriter you will often say things like: 'I don't think someone would do or think that.' Your job is not about making people do what you want them to do, but helping them do what they want to do.

It can be tricky to get people to trust that they're not necessarily the best person to write the content. That can be a bit awkward – but it's because they might be too close to the information and not be able to think like the target audience.

Copy is often thought of as the last thing to go into a website or app but actually a copywriter also thinks about what information should go where. Getting into the design process early enough to have an impact can be a problem and you end up having to write a certain number of words to fit into a box so it doesn't 'break the design'. Eye-roll. If someone's using a screen reader the design won't matter anyway.

Another challenge is that copy can't fix behind-the-scenes process problems and it shouldn't have to explain the design. It's not a plaster and sometimes you will have to balance being the voice of the user with managing the expectations of your client.

Storytelling

At the heart of most great writing is storytelling. It's something humans have been doing since we learnt to paint on cave walls or hold forth around the fire. We naturally respond to powerful stories that capture our imagination. When writing, it's easy to emphasize the facts – how much something cost, its features, why something needs to change, the people involved and so on. Naturally, it's right and proper that some writing only sticks to the facts. You'd be very surprised if you went to pay your tax online and were presented with a powerful story about tax officials.

But by ignoring the power of storytelling, much writing fails to reach or influence many people. When people share pieces on social media they are doing so because of an emotional response. The content has made them feel happy, sad, angry or proud. By telling a powerful story, you're raising the odds of people sharing it with others as it's more likely to create an emotional response.

Storytelling is a fundamental part of journalism. I've never met a reporter who doesn't care about telling powerful stories based on factual investigation. It's also a fundamental part of other forms of communication. In marketing, when there is a powerful narrative or story behind a product or individual, it means that audiences are more likely to remember it. Think of the two Steves building the first Apple computer in their garage. If you want to work in marketing or advertising, you will find that by creating a compelling story your audiences will be a lot more interested in what you have to say. Storytelling is another skill that takes practice, so don't neglect it when planning what you want to learn or develop.

Storytelling is also important for whole organizations. Businesses and charities don't just spring out of the ground. Why were they created? Who were the people behind them? What do they care about? A powerful organizational story helps them stand out in a world of near-unlimited digital content and brands. By sharing this story you create a clear identity that others can understand as well as people within your organization. This can then be used as the base for your branding and tone of voice.

Press releases

A press release is a short written document sent to journalists to promote something in the hope they will cover it. It could be an event, a product or policy announcement, or a good set of financial results. It will have all the important information the journalist needs as well as contacts if they want to find out more. They also try to make the material sound as exciting as possible to make it stand out in the busy journalist's e-mail inbox. They are usually sent out by PR companies or departments.

It's recently become quite fashionable to say the press release is dead. Organizations or individuals can use social media to speak directly to the public rather than having to try to get coverage from news organizations. And journalists are now looking for a mix of content from PR professionals rather than just a few written paragraphs. News organizations want their digital articles to include video or photographic content as well as writing.

Still, press releases remain valuable. Most journalists will complain about being hounded by PRs (often calling them 'flacks'), but a good relationship between a journalist and PR is very useful to both sides.

A press release is still a useful document for a journalist to refer to. It's handy to have information for a story to base the writing on. The contacts, product or event information is very useful. They often feature embargos so the journalist can prepare a story but not publish sensitive information too early. In the digital age embargos are becoming less relevant as they are a hangover from the newspaper print deadline days. Digital publishers no longer have many deadlines and simply publish 24/7.

If you do need to write a press release here are some general pointers:

- The headline should be attention-grabbing but not deceptive. If journalists think your press releases are frequently deceptive, they will simply start ignoring you.

- Include as much useful information as possible, but don't pad it out with marketing speak or hyperbole.

- Include contacts for interested journalists to find out more information if they need to.

- Include a mix of content too. Journalists are more likely to run the story on their digital platforms if it includes easy-to-download video clips or high-quality photos.

The principles of plain English and brevity definitely still apply to press releases, so keep the language and subject matter tight while writing them. A suggested structure is:

An effective headline This captures people's attention and sums up the pitch in one sentence. Make sure you include any embargo information too.

The story – who, what, why, when, where and how? The main body of the press release should cover the details clearly and without marketing speak. Be clear about what the news value is – why is this story interesting to journalists?

Quotes It can be useful to include quotes from relevant high-level people that can be used in the piece. Often these can be quite lengthy, so keep them concise and interesting.

Contact details Include your contact details in case the journalist has further questions or would like to discuss the story.

Content Publishers are under pressure to include photos and video in each article they write. Include easy-to-download links to content, as it will increase the odds of journalists using it.

Creating a style guide

Having a clear style also does wonders for branding. It's easy just to think of fonts, colours and logos when considering how to brand a product or organization. The style of language used is often forgotten but just as important. Let's go back to my edible sticky tape example:

Epic burgers need powerful hold! Edible sticky tape – buy it NOW

The perfect little gadget to keep your lunch lovely

Edible sticky tape helps keep your lunch safe and secure

It's the same product but each example makes it sound very different. For the individual, understanding how language can change mood and meaning makes them more employable. You may work at very different organizations in your career, and being able to adapt quickly to their written tone of voice is a valuable skill to have.

If you're managing a team of communicators, they will need guidance on what written tone of voice is right for the organization. This chapter covered style guides earlier, but here are some simple tips to get started:

- *Use the active voice rather than the passive.* By saying 'I wrote the book' rather than 'the book was written by me', your language is clearer and more engaging.

- *Describe your audience.* It can be useful to create fictitious people who represent the audiences you want to reach. Thinking about how you would write and speak to them can help your team understand why tone of voice matters.

- *Keep it simple.* Don't use complicated or pompous words. Just explain things as clearly as possible. So 'Ensure your workstation computer is elevated comfortably' becomes 'Your computer should be at a comfortable height.'

- *Don't bully your audience.* Instead of lecturing them, explain why something is worth reading. No one likes to be bullied. 'You must watch this video about human rights now' should be 'This human rights video shows why they are so important.'

Individual social media pages are often run by huge teams of people. If you look at those belonging to big brands, you (should) see that all the posts sound as if they are written by the same person. This is because they have very clear brand style guides as well as the resources to employ people just to check each post for consistency. It's not something most organizations and, of course, individuals can do.

When you have different people working on the same channel, it's easy for their own writing styles, bad habits and idiosyncrasies to 'leak' through into the posts they publish. Therefore having a style guide for people to refer to means a much more consistent tone of voice without the need for lots of expensive copy-editors.

There are many style guides out there to base yours on and learn from. Everyone who writes for a living has their favourites and they can often be the source of fierce debate. Most major news organizations have their own style guides and they often update readers on how they are changing over time. If there's a particular publisher you love to read, see if they publish their own style guide as they can be fantastic sources to learn from.

Common mistakes

Clickbait

Just don't do it. Clickbait is the name given to intentionally eye-catching and misleading headlines or social media posts. As the name suggests, they are designed to get people clicking on to the story. The websites behind them do this because they rely on advertising revenue based on the amount of clicks they get rather than the time people spend reading a story. So they will post lurid photos with misleading headlines on social media and not care that people are often disappointed and leave the website quickly.

There can often be a fine line between a teasing digital headline and clickbait. If you are being intentionally misleading, deliberately mysterious or sensationalist, it's clickbait. Great digital content should give people a valid reason for wanting to find out more from a story rather than tricking them into clicking on it.

Some examples of clickbait are:

The one amazing weight loss trick you've never heard of (a link to a website selling useless pills)

This photo of two cops is going viral for a stunning reason (they are working at Christmas)

Look what a shock these celebrities got when they went out for dinner (someone took a photo of them).

Jargon

Avoid jargon at all costs – especially meaningless business speak. It can often be insidious, so keep a close eye out for it. Phrases like 'going forward', 'ideation', 'align', 'actionable', 'sunset a product', 'granular leverage' and so on are useless and dull to read. If you're trying to get someone's attention and give them a clear message, business speak is the worst way to do it.

Robot speak

This is similar to jargon but instead of meaningless phrases it is just very dry, formal, stuffy language that complicates the message. This tends to be used by big organizations that aren't used to speaking to the public directly. For example:

'This firm has recently received instruction to act on behalf of Mr John Smith in regards to the matter set out below' rather than just saying 'We act for Mr John Smith.'

'This technology allows your organization to enhance its sales capability by providing detailed customer behaviour data' rather than just saying 'This technology helps you understand your customer.'

Exercise

For this exercise, come up with two subjects. One of them should be something you are absolutely passionate about, which you can speak about at length. The other should be the dullest thing you can think of.

For each one, write:

1 an exciting, accurate headline about that subject;

2 a 400-word summary of that subject;

3 a longer-form 1,200-word piece of storytelling about that subject.

While writing, remember the importance of the reader understanding everything clearly. Keep asking yourself whether what you are writing would be clear to someone who knows nothing about it. You could go further – would a caveman understand this?

Once you have done this exercise for both the subject you care about and the one you find dull, show them to someone who ideally doesn't know anything about either one. Ask them:

1 Did they understand it?

2 Did you make it sound interesting?

3 What could you have changed?

It's also worth thinking carefully about the writing process. What did you find hard and easy for each one? Where did you struggle? What skills do you need to improve?

Now you've identified your strengths and weaknesses, you can create an action plan to improve the skills you're not confident with and promote your strengths. With writing, it does take practice, so do try this exercise regularly. You can also find examples of writing you enjoy and think carefully about what it is that makes them so interesting. There are also plenty of blogs and forums where writers share tips and advice that can be very useful.

Summary

In this chapter we have covered the importance of plain English, avoiding jargon, and why a tone of voice is important. Writing is something that many people love doing. But it can terrify others, especially when they are writing content that is meant for the public.

Writing takes patience and practice. Thankfully, it's something you can practise at any time without any special tools or tutors. Keep your writing skills sharp, as most jobs you have will need them.

Finally, remember that a powerful phrase or story can be more effective than the most lavishly produced video or beautifully taken photo. When you're working with digital content, don't overlook the words.

Making great video 03

- Video is an essential type of content to produce.
- It's easier and cheaper than you may think.
- Live video is important too.

Billy Joel's *52nd Street* was the first commercially released album on compact disc. When CDs first came out, customers were promised fantastic sound quality like they had never heard before. Unfortunately, many albums were still being mastered with vinyl in mind, meaning many CD albums actually sounded very bad. Thankfully, record labels soon realized their mistake and started mastering for compact disc too.

Although things are getting better, many organizations treat video for digital in a similar way. Most digital video is watched on a smartphone with the sound switched off (about 85 per cent of the time, according to Digiday, a digital industry news site). A four-minute TV news package with lots of people talking in it isn't going to work well. Understanding how producing for digital platforms is different from other kinds of video is a fundamental skill of any digital creative.

What do we mean by digital video? You could argue it's any video watched on an internet-connected device. But then surely that means films and documentaries on Netflix count as digital video?

You could choose to define it as video watched on social media. But this is also unhelpful as it ignores dedicated video websites such as YouTube or Vimeo.

I choose to define it as video designed to be watched on smartphones. This is because:

1 The majority of internet usage is now on a mobile device (according to StatCounter Global Stats, desktop was overtaken in 2016).

2 Social media and dedicated video sites get the vast majority of traffic from mobile devices (in 2016 Facebook got 92.7 per cent of its monthly active users from mobile).

3 Video designed for mobiles is very different from video designed for televisions, so it's important to produce them differently.

Desktop and tablet viewing shouldn't be ignored, but the stats show that it's beneficial to focus on producing video content that works best for mobile, as that is how it will largely be viewed.

It might seem strange to think that most digital video is watched with the sound off. That's until you consider people's habits. They are often browsing on their phone quickly, probably in a public place, at work or listening to music. They can watch video, but turning the sound on might interrupt their music or start rudely playing out of their phones. It would also be very annoying to browse networks that automatically play video with all that sound blaring at you. People prefer to watch with the sound off and then switch it on if they are interested.

Video is one of the most popular kinds of digital content and there are very few social networks that don't support it in some way. Making video used to mean going to an expensive production company with high-end cameras and edit suites. Now, cheaper equipment and easier-to-use tools mean more people and organizations can create it themselves than ever before.

Smartphones also allow people to record incredibly good-quality video as well as editing and sharing it with the world. Live video means people can broadcast events instantly to anyone they want. So when thinking of digital video we shouldn't just think of pre-recorded, edited video but live, raw video too.

While the technical production of video is now much easier, the craft of storytelling and production is still something that you need to learn. Just as how everyone with a phone camera isn't a brilliant photographer, not everyone pressing the record button will be able to make great video.

But great video absolutely does not mean highly polished, over-produced, formal video. It can seem daunting, but producing it is easier than you may think. A ten-second wobbly smartphone video of something fascinating is still a brilliant video – no one will care that it wasn't colour corrected or shot without a tripod.

In this chapter we will cover how to make a great digital video and why it's a very valuable skill to have. We'll look at the differences between traditional and digital video, some suggestions about what equipment you can use, and examine the craft of storytelling through video. You will also learn about some of the more recent formats such as 360 video.

Don't feel that video is too complicated to learn. I learnt by borrowing cameras and playing around with editing apps. If I can do it without any lessons, anyone can.

Why video is essential

Video content is the most popular kind over photography and writing on digital platforms. Cisco predicts it will account for 82 per cent of all consumer traffic by 2020. It's also given massive priority by the social networks – they simply want their users to upload as much video as possible.

Why?

There are a number of reasons other than the fact that video is popular with audiences. In a busy newsfeed, moving images get people's attention. If you use a social network, have a quick scroll through its feed. You'll notice your eye naturally gets drawn to the videos that start automatically playing. This makes video a useful tool in getting the audience's attention.

Video allows you to explain complicated subjects easily in an entertaining way. It's a worrying statistic, but the average adult's reading age is that of a young child. Half of the UK's adult working population have a reading age of 11 or younger, according to the Office of National Statistics. In the previous chapter you read about the importance of plain English. While writing in that way will help, many people still struggle with reading, and even confident readers will be bored by lengthy instructions or explanations. Therefore a video allows you to explain a concept or story quickly. Being able to include visual examples gives visuals an advantage over text.

There are also commercial reasons. Most publishers rely on advertising for their business. Video 'pre-roll' adverts (those that automatically play before the video) tend to create a lot more money for publishers than website banner adverts. So there's a big incentive for them to publish as much video as possible.

'Publishers' includes any organization that produces content for an audience. News organizations, radio stations, government departments – they are all publishers on digital. If you want to work for a publisher, having video skills means you can help them pay the bills. If you want to work in marketing or PR, you can offer your product video to organizations you want to promote your product. They would then be more likely to cover your announcement.

Most publishers used to specialize in one type of content. It's stating the obvious, but TV channels just produced video, newspapers just produced print, and so on. With digital platforms everyone can publish a range of content. You may be writing a story, but most digital writing platforms let you combine it with photos and video clips. Most articles now online will have a mix of photos, videos, audio and text.

It's not just video that an organization produces itself that's valuable. Most people now carry an HD camera around in their pockets – their phones. You can ask your audience to share their clips for a news story, footage from an event or their thoughts and opinions.

Live video gives everyone with a phone enormous power and reach. In 2016, Facebook announced its new live feature allowing anyone to broadcast to the world from their phone. This means learning not just how to produce digital video, but also how to produce and plan effective live video too.

The differences between linear and digital video

Linear video is content produced for what some think of as traditional platforms – television, DVDs, news reports. These are commonly called linear because they are scheduled rather than chosen or found by the viewer. It's probably easier just to keep the biggest difference in mind – linear video is produced for a large widescreen TV with people sitting watching it. Linear video is often watched in a way called 'appointment to view'. This means people know what time it is on and make a conscious decision to sit down and watch it. Think of that TV programme you like watching every Sunday night or the big sports match coming up.

Digital video is usually watched on a smartphone, meaning a smaller, vertical screen. It's also largely watched with the sound off, as mentioned earlier. People often find video in their social media newsfeeds, which means they are distracted and can quickly scroll past if it doesn't interest them.

Some quick main practical differences between the two are:

Linear video

1 Longer in length – from 30-second TV adverts to 5-minute news reports to 60-minute feature-length programmes.

2 Highly produced – audiences don't like watching raw footage for a long time, so it will be polished and carefully put together.

3 Takes time to tell a story – as people will be watching for longer, the video has a slower narrative arc.

4 Sound is very important – as much attention is paid to the music, dialogue and sound effects as to the visuals.

5 Builds up to a big finish – linear video producers want people to watch for as long as possible, so they usually save the best stuff until the end.

6 Designed for a large screen – widescreen video with detailed shots/ graphics.

Digital video

1 Very short – busy people with lots of things to look at on their phones won't spend long watching videos, so digital video is usually very short and concise. Between 10 and 30 seconds is usual.

2 Silent – most digital video will be watched with the sound switched off, so bold text or subtitles are often used in place of a voiceover.

3 Designed for a phone screen – vertical or square video with graphics large enough to read on a small screen works best.

4 Powerful introduction – the good footage needs to be at the start of the video to capture people's attention in a busy feed.

5 Raw (sometimes) – while a lot of digital video is very professional, raw video also does very well. Think of funny clips on YouTube or live broadcasts from a phone. Success with digital video can be measured as simply the number of views, or using more detailed statistics such as the length of time people watched for, how many shares the video got or how many people who saw it commented.

Confusingly, digital video can also be made up of mixed media. By taking a few still images, animating them and then adding some text, you then have a digital video. While linear video does often feature photos (documentaries especially), 60 minutes of them would be extremely boring. This means you can easily produce video products with just a couple of photos and some text.

Having these main differences to hand means that while you might not be producing video yourself, you know what to ask for when commissioning video.

The types of digital video

While the points made earlier should act as a general guide, there are obviously differences when producing video for different purposes. A journalistic explainer video and an advert can both be vertical and silent, but their subject matter and style will be very different indeed. Here are some examples of the different types of video and their differences. You can use these examples to think about what sort you would like to produce and, in turn, what jobs you want to do.

Journalistic

News organizations use both raw and produced videos, with an unsurprising focus on the story and events occurring in the footage rather than necessarily quality. The rise of live video on social media has also been a boon for journalists and citizens alike, as anyone can share footage of a breaking news event instantly. Live videos can also be used by journalists to interview or answer questions from the public about a news event.

Often the role of journalism is to explain complex or controversial issues as clearly and objectively as possible. Explainer videos are popular. These are short, concise videos that explain a complex topic. They often use graphics and animation to further illustrate the subject. If you want to produce these sorts of video, look at examples from the major news organizations and try using an animation app such as After Effects to reproduce it for yourself.

Long-form video documentaries and storytelling have also seen a resurgence on digital platforms. This content takes a lot of skill to produce, but don't be dissuaded. To keep the viewer watching for the full programme, you must tell a compelling and unique story. With digital, you can also combine the video with other sorts of content, such as interactive photo galleries or written excerpts.

Content marketing

Perhaps the most famous example of content marketing is the launch video from Dollar Shave Club. They are a subscription razor company that entered into a competitive market with very large, powerful incumbents dominating most of the market share.

They produced a hilarious video, with the CEO explaining why their blades are worth buying in terms that probably aren't best written down in this book. At the time of writing it has 24 million views.

By producing content that people actually wanted to watch rather than adverts, they reached far larger audiences, people actively shared their video and they quickly built up a business. Content marketing can be hard, though, as it isn't easy producing great, entertaining video that people actually want to watch while selling to them. Humour or appealing to emotion is often the best way to succeed, so this could be a good route if you are interested in marketing and have a knack for funny, attention-grabbing ideas.

Personal brand building

Many people have made a career out of video blogging. Perhaps the most famous of these are PewDiePie and Zoella, who have enormous audiences and command large sums of money to feature products or brands in their videos. For many young people, their celebrities are video bloggers rather than media stars.

If there is a cause or subject you care strongly about, you can share your thoughts with the world. The technical side of producing this video is easy – often a computer's webcam will do the trick. The hard part is producing video that's compelling, but most important of all, content that's authentic.

Personal brand building can also be a useful way to help boost your career prospects. If you want to advance in an industry you already work in, you can produce videos where you give advice, share your thoughts on what's happening in the industry and answer questions from people. You'll build up your reputation and be seen as a leader within your field.

Education

In the public and charitable sectors there is often a need to explain important announcements in an interesting and informative way. For example, a government stop-smoking scheme would need videos and animations to explain the risks of smoking and the support available to people.

These videos, like journalistic explainers, often rely on animation and text, so building up your animation skills is also valuable for these industries. Condensing a complex subject into a minute or two can be hard and will take practice.

A video that does this well is 'Dumb Ways to Die'. It went viral around the world despite being created for Metro Trains in Australia. Admittedly it was produced by an advertising agency, but it shows the power of video content used well to convey an important public service message.

Creative

Obviously, all content production is creative, but you may wish to specialize in fictional or narrative content. The ease with which people can produce video content combined with free distribution online means there has never been a better time to produce creative video. You can also get advice and ideas from online communities.

The video itself is entirely your vision and there are few constraints on what you can do. The advice to keep in mind would be the importance of not just producing creative video but promoting your video too. The accessibility you can benefit from also means there are lots of people producing video out there, so you'll need to 'shout' online if you want to be heard.

Make sure you keep an eye on what other people are producing for ideas and inspiration. There are wonderful short films being produced all over the world that are shared on video sites designed for creatives, such as Vimeo. They can provide you with a never-ending source of inspiration.

The skills you (and your team) need

There is a range of skills you or your team will need in order to produce great video for digital. This is not an exhaustive list, but by having these basics you'll be able to produce high-quality video easily.

Planning

For anything other than the simplest of shoots you'll always need to plan ahead of time. This would include:

- Storyboard your shoot to plan what shots you want to get ahead of time and get an idea of what the end video will look like. This can be on paper, with crude drawings, or on a storyboarding app. There are plenty of free apps out there and they will make your shoot a lot smoother. Storyboarding forces you to visualize exactly what the video will look like and gives you an idea of how the video will look. If you don't feel confident doing this, you can try 'reverse storyboarding' one of your favourite film scenes.

- Logistics are important for any kind of shoot. Have you booked the equipment you need? Do you have the permission you need to film in the location you want to use? Is everyone who needs to be there briefed on when to arrive? And never forget to check your camera batteries. Make a checklist of all the tasks that need doing and stick to it. Often tools such as Trello or Evernote can be useful for keeping you organized. It's also worth reviewing these lists once you have finished. What was missed out? What mistakes were made in the planning?

- Post-production – once the filming is finished, how will you get the footage edited and distributed? You could do this yourself at your desk, or do you need to book a dedicated editor? It's also worth thinking about what the 'sign-off' process is for the video. Who needs to approve it and how long will that take? The storyboard you made is again useful as it gives you a rough guide to edit to. You shouldn't feel as if you have to rigidly stick to it as you may prefer different shots, but it gives you a structure to follow as you begin putting the video together.

So, while producing video is creative and a lot of fun, you still need to have organizational skills. Planning will reduce the amount of things that can go wrong and will help you relax about a complicated shoot. Make sure you never let over-planning get in the way of a good shoot. If you have a very limited window of time to film something, just get on with it and hope for the best.

Camera

Video can be produced on anything from a smartphone to professional cameras. Digital producers should be comfortable producing video on either. The main camera skills to build up are:

- Camera set-up – know how to set up your camera for different shots. For example, a moving shot of a landscape will need a tripod while a gig in a dark room will need low light settings switched on.

- Filming sequences – you want your shots to flow together. Don't just randomly film lots of pretty shots – they should have a logical sequence. For example, imagine a house. A sequence would be a distant shot outside showing the whole building, then a closer shot of the door, then a close-up of the door handle with someone's hand holding and turning it. This will make your final video a lot more interesting to watch.

- Interviewing – producers will often have to interview someone for a video. There's the technical side to setting up interview shots:

using lights, setting up the microphones and making sure the guest is comfortable. The producer also needs interpersonal skills to get the best interview they can. Guests are often nervous and it takes coaxing to get the best performance you can out of them.

Editing

Editing is the process of putting your filmed material together. You'll also need editing skills to put other people's content together or for animating photos into a video sequence. There are a few main editing apps out there, but once you know one it's often quite easy to switch over to another. Currently the most popular are Avid, Adobe Premiere and Final Cut Pro.

Try to get access to one of these editing apps and practise. They can look intimidating at first, but there are lots of helpful 'how to' videos online that can get you started. They can be expensive and need a powerful computer too, so you could find a university or college that has editing machines or try to get work experience in a post-production company.

You should build up your skills in three stages:

1 Learn simply to cut video footage into sequences. Take some raw footage, cut the material you don't need and turn it into a shorter video.
2 Learn how to do more complex editing by adding music, title screens, and photos. By learning these skills you will be ready to produce video professionally.
3 If you want to take your skills further, it's worth learning how you can use apps like After Effects to add advanced titles and effects to your video. These apps can be complicated, but again there are plenty of resources online.

Graphic design

It might sound odd to say graphic design is an important skill for video. But you'll often have to produce smart-looking titles and 'cover photos' to promote your video online, and understand the fundamentals of design. By having an eye for good design your videos will look more professional and appealing to the audience.

You don't need to be able to produce professional graphics, but learn the basics of good design. There are many good books and guides out there and it will make your video look much better.

Editorial

Editorial judgement is the most important skill a journalist can have, but it's important for any role that involves making content for the public. It's judging whether the video is appropriate for the audience, if it's sensible to put out in the current news environment, or if the story is worth publishing. It's obviously a lot more important for non-fiction video rather than creative.

Let's go back to my edible sticky tape example. The social media team have prepared a brilliant video to announce the launch of edible sticky tape. It sounds like content that wouldn't be controversial in any way. But on the morning of the launch a major report is published saying the production of sticky tape is responsible for environmental damage. In the video there are plenty of shots of people using sticky tape at picnics, surrounded by trees. Editorially it would be bad to put out the video at this time.

Editorial skills are especially important when producing video. With the huge number of visuals you can easily be tripped up.

This is not a comprehensive checklist, but it's worth asking yourself these questions:

1 Does this video accurately depict both sides of a story or issue?

2 Does the video misrepresent the facts or what people have said?

3 Does the current news agenda affect how this video would be perceived by the audience?

4 Did the people filmed in the video give consent for their footage to be used in this way?

5 Is anyone's copyright infringed by this video?

Presenting skills

If the people producing the video are also good at recording voice-overs or presenting on camera, they become one-person production companies. It's worth identifying who performs well on camera and using them in your videos. Sometimes having a charismatic presenter makes video more engaging, and they can often explain or demonstrate a concept more clearly than text.

Obviously, very few people indeed will excel at all of these skills, but it's worth having at least a basic understanding of each one. If you're building a team, you can mix and match staff that are complementary to one another.

The equipment you (and your team) need

Producing video used to be very expensive owing to the vast amount of professional equipment needed. Thankfully, professional video can now be produced much more cheaply and easily.

Here is a suggested list of equipment you will need. It's easy to feel overwhelmed by the vast amount of gadgets available, but this list covers the basics. Before you go on a shopping spree, though, remember that you can produce incredible video with just your smartphone. It's a great way to practise video production without any cost to you. A list of suggested equipment you can purchase is included later in the chapter.

Cameras

You can get excellent-quality cameras for around £1,000. These are usually either dedicated video cameras or DSLRs (digital single lens reflex cameras, or in other words, photographic cameras). DSLRs have become very popular for video production as they give a very cinematic look to the video owing to the powerful lens. As these are designed for mainly taking photos, though, you often have to get used to some quirks when shooting video, for example no microphone. If you already have a DSLR, experiment with its video mode.

When purchasing a dedicated video camera, check it has the following features:

- Does it have a big enough internal hard drive to shoot plenty of footage? If it records to cards, make sure you buy enough spares to last you a whole shoot.
- Can you easily plug in accessories such as professional microphones, lights and so on?
- Does it fit on standard tripods?
- Is it solidly built? Filming often means the camera will get knocked and bumped, so it's important it's robust enough to survive your creative plans.
- Are the batteries easily swappable? Some cameras have built-in batteries that may appear more convenient, but if you're on a lengthy shoot you'll be in big trouble if they runs out.

Tripod

A tripod allows you to steady your shot. This is especially important for interviews and close-up detailed shots. They range massively in price from the very cheap (£30-ish) to the immensely expensive (£1,000+).

Unsurprisingly, the most important factor is how sturdy and stable the tripod is. If you'll be filming on the move a lot, you'll want to get something more portable.

Microphones

One thing all cameras have in common is that their built-in microphones are all absolutely awful. A proper microphone is therefore essential. There are a number of different types of microphone, so think about what you're likely to need:

- *Handheld microphones* are usually used by presenters and reporters. They are quick, easy and effective, but look incredibly odd if they are used by anyone other than a presenter. You can also add branding to them.

- *Lavalier microphones* are often called clip or lapel mics. These are small microphones that clip to the interviewee's jacket and are often used in studios or for interviews. They look very subtle and connect to the camera wirelessly, so they are very useful if someone is speaking far away from the camera.

- *Shotgun microphones* range in size from small ones that sit on top of the camera to the large ones on the end of poles used on film sets. These are good all-rounders and are quite cheap.

Lighting

Without any lighting kit you're completely at the mercy of the light where you're shooting. A moodily lit bar can look incredibly dark on camera, so invest in some lighting equipment. You can get good small lights that attach to the top of your camera, but they can make your subject look paparazzi'd. However, full-size lights are very large and fragile, so they can be difficult to carry around with you. There are many different types, so consider:

1 What type of light do you want? If you're filming a creative video, you may want ones that replicate natural light. If, on the other hand, you are a news reporter, you may simply want a powerful light that illuminates as much as possible.

2 How portable do you want the kit to be?

3 How tall do you want the lights to be? You'll want them to come up to head height if you often interview people, which means sacrificing portability.

A small, cheap light on top of your camera is better than nothing, so it's a good idea to carry one in your kit bag.

Headphones

Without headphones you will have no idea if the audio levels are right for your video. The microphones could be too loud, or the person speaking may be too quiet. Without headphones you'll have to wait until you sit down to edit the video to find out if the levels are correct, and you may be in for a nasty shock.

Edit computer and software

Once you've finished filming, you'll need to edit the video. You will need a fairly powerful computer to do this on, as editing can take up a lot of power, especially from the video card. It can be a laptop or a desktop computer, but make sure it's powerful enough. If you're just doing very simple editing, most machines will be able to do it, but if you start animating or working with multiple channels of very high-quality video, it will struggle. Check it has an above-average video card and RAM (random access memory), as these will be the most important features of an edit machine.

Optional extras

Here are some extra pieces of kit that may be useful:

- *Action cameras such as GoPro* are small and cube-shaped and can be attached to virtually anything using special accessories. They are very popular with extreme sports fans who can wear them while snowboarding or skydiving. They are not expensive and are incredibly versatile.

- *Drones* allow you to record stunning aerial shots. In the past, you needed to hire a helicopter to record the kind of shots you can now get with a drone for a few hundred pounds. Many countries require you to have a licence to operate them, though, so make sure you are qualified to use one.

- *360 cameras* record video in a sphere that people can then move as they watch. Like action cameras, they are not too expensive and create interactive videos. You can also attach them to a drone for interactive 360 video. These are commonly used for video designed for virtual reality headsets.

- *Different lenses* are important for any DSLR filming you do. DSLRs have different lenses that you'll need to change depending on the shot. So you may want to film something very close-up in minute detail followed by a wide-angle shot of a landscape.

- *Dolly kits* allow you to film smooth horizontal motion. While there are small kits out there, they are still quite big to carry around. Dolly shots do look very professional, so it may be worthwhile.

Smartphone kit

If you do decide to stick with your smartphone to produce video, there are a few pieces of equipment that are worth buying to improve the quality of your video:

- *Camera lenses* that attach to the back of your phone and improve the quality of the shot.
- *Handheld Steadicams* make your shot more stable. The more advanced ones also have features such as face tracking, which can be useful if you're doing an interview. These are especially good for live video.
- *Battery boosters* are essential, as smartphone batteries are woefully underpowered and shooting video drains them quickly, especially if it's live.
- *Tripods* are also useful for interviews and pieces to camera. There are plenty that are designed specifically for smartphones.
- *Signal boosters* are vital for any live videos you want to broadcast where there isn't Wi-Fi.
- *Microphones* give a big advantage over the built-in microphones on your phone.

Live video

Live video has exploded in popularity over the past few years, especially with the launch of Periscope and Facebook Live. Anyone can now broadcast live to the world from their phones. It's popular with audiences as it feels more authentic than a pre-produced video, they can interact with the people in the video and they will usually watch for longer.

Live video does have its own opportunities and challenges, however. The most obvious one is that, being live, you have much less control over it while it's being broadcast. Despite this, live video is an essential type of content that you should produce. If you have a complicated subject to explain, get the same questions from your audience or are hosting an event, live video is usually the best choice.

Many news publishers, like the BBC, host regular live Q&A with their journalists where their followers can ask for more information about the big news stories. Many publishers are also scheduling broadcasts at the same time each night in order to create an 'appointment to view', much like TV programmes.

So what are the advantages and disadvantages of live video? And how do you avoid mistakes?

The advantages of live video are:

- Social networks are promoting it heavily, which means your live videos will reach a much larger audience than other types of content.

- It allows your audience to interact with you. They can ask questions, share their opinions and see what other people have to say. When planning a live video, make sure it's as interactive as possible, with the people on camera ready to respond to comments and questions.

- It's more authentic. In a world of unlimited content, live video stands out as being immediate and unfiltered. Many make the mistake of thinking that good digital video means as slickly produced as possible. The reality is it should be as authentic as possible, and live video allows you to do this easily.

- It can very quickly go viral, as people can share live video with their friends instantly. If what's being broadcast is powerful video, people will share it very quickly.

What are the drawbacks of live video?

- You have less control as it is, of course, going out immediately. This can worry a lot of people. Prep the people on camera beforehand, make sure you have as much control as possible of where you're filming, but overall just relax. The audience knows it's a live video and is different to a pre-produced one.

- It feels more informal than a sit-down interview with a camera. Some people who aren't aware of live video can feel baffled or underwhelmed when you set up a shoot only to point a smartphone at them. Explain why the video is important and why you don't need any big, complex pieces of equipment.

- If you don't have a Wi-Fi connection, you are at the mercy of the local phone signal. A poor signal means bad-quality video or not even being able to do a live video at all. You can mitigate this by setting up your own hot spot or buying a signal booster.

CASE STUDY Vivek Kemp, CNN International

Vivek Kemp is Executive Producer at CNN Digital Worldwide. CNN in October 2016 had 447 million video starts and has built a reputation for creativity and powerful journalistic storytelling.

I never really knew what I wanted to do for a living. I had worked in retail, but had zero sense of a career. That changed on a backpacking trip to Central America. I had been documenting all of my adventures in a journal and then one day, at an internet café in Guatemala, I leaned over to a friend of mine and said, 'I think I want to go Columbia University and get a journalism degree.'

I had zero idea about the media world, but I knew I wanted to write and I loved telling stories. After I graduated with a master's degree in print in 2005, I got a post as features reporter for *The Naples Daily News*, covering everything from a voodoo priest to Marilyn Manson's talents as a water-colour painter. Florida is a great place to find an odd story. After two and a half years at the paper it became obvious that the growth in media was in digital, and even if you were a writer you needed to know how to produce video as well.

While I dreamed of writing for *Esquire* in New York, I knew that if I was going to get a foot in the NYC media world I needed to know how to shoot, edit and report a news story in any format – print, audio, video. With that in mind, I quit the newspaper and got a job as an assignment editor at NBC Network News on the international desk. While my days were spent monitoring breaking news behind a desk, I borrowed a video camera on my days off and taught myself to shoot and edit. Eventually I started pitching stories to shows. Those skills set me up to become videographer/producer for a News Corp. start-up called The Daily. After a couple extraordinary years producing hundreds of high-end original stories, I jumped ship to *Fast Company* magazine to build their video department. Then three years ago CNN approached me.

I should note that I've never owned a camera – I think learning video is as hard as you make it. If you really want to learn something, you'll find a way. I've been lucky enough to come into contact with people who like to encourage passion. That's as true now as it was when I was younger. Producers never had to take the time to hand me a camera and say Go try something new – but they did.

The power of digital media is that there are so many ways to tell a story, whether it's a video, an infographic, a photo gallery or an article – it's about choosing your path and using it to its full potential.

Common mistakes

Here are some common mistakes people often make when producing digital video.

Lengthy introductions

How many videos have you seen that start with a logo? Then five seconds later, a title screen. Then after another five seconds there's another title. By then, 95 per cent of the audience will have stopped watching without seeing any of the actual video.

With digital video you must start with a compelling, powerful shot that captures the audience's attention. If they are scrolling through a social media newsfeed, they have plenty to look at and you'll have to get their attention.

Thinking TV

That lavish, widescreen, six-minute TV advert your company spent a lot of money producing isn't going to work well on digital platforms at all. Remember, most people will be watching on a phone, so ideally the video should be square or vertical. Overly polished video will also often not work well if it's for marketing. If you're storytelling, stunning imagery is important, but keep the shots as clear and uncluttered as possible to make them 'sing' on the small screen people will be watching on.

Not planning for silence

With digital video you will rely on text and subtitles to tell the story more than for broadcast video production. Most digital video is watched with the sound off, so you'll need to use subtitles wherever there's speech.

Overthinking it

If you have a great piece of video that's quite raw, shaky or different but is still very compelling, it's still worth sharing with your audience. You can also easily overthink your planning. Of course, being prepared helps ensure your shoot goes smoothly, but as German military strategist Helmuth von Moltke said: 'No battle plan survives contact with the enemy.' Stuff is bound to go wrong or not work out as planned, but focus on producing the most interesting video you can by whatever means necessary and you're bound to be fine.

Exercise

This is an exercise in two parts. The first part you can do at any time, but I recommend you give it a go straight away. For the second part you can use standard video and editing equipment, but don't feel discouraged if you don't have access to any. You can use your smartphone as described earlier in the chapter.

Part one

Look on your social media feeds and save a few videos that catch your eye. What interested you about them? How do you think the producers made them? They could have carefully produced a video on a formal shoot or just shared a smartphone video.

Also think about what was the emotional hook that made you watch the video. Was it funny? Moving? Did you learn something new?

You should also do this for in-depth storytelling. Look at journalistic documentaries online that interest you and again try to work out what the narrative arc is, what planning and equipment they would have needed, and of course what it is about the content that interests you.

Once you've done this a few times you'll start noticing patterns emerging. You can use this information to think about what kinds of video interest you and how easy they were to make. You can then use this information to plan what sort of video you want to try producing.

You can then move on to part two if you can get access to the equipment you need. If you aren't sure, you can try contacting local colleges that have video production kit and see if you can visit them.

Part two

Once you have access to some basic camera and editing equipment, try producing some simple videos. These suggestions give you a good range of subjects/types of video and once you're more confident you can build up a strong portfolio of videos to show to potential employers:

- *An interview.* Find someone with an interesting story to tell, sit them down and record an interview with them. You'll have a lot of footage, so you'll then need to cut it down into a video a few minutes long. This will give you experience in setting up a simple shoot but also test your editorial judgement. What do you keep in? Is the narrative clear throughout the video?

- *Someone making a coffee.* It may sound strange, but at a local café ask if you can film them making a coffee. The reason for this is that it will teach you the importance of filming sequences of shots that follow a logical order. It's also a nice visual process, allowing you to get lots of creative shots and then edit them into a smart video. You can always give the video to the café as a gift too!

- *An explainer.* In the previous exercises you have had to explain something complicated as simply as possible. Now your challenge is to explain something complicated using video. Carefully plan how best to tell the story. Should you interview someone? Use graphics perhaps? You may have to plan a shoot to get additional footage. This will get you planning your shoot much more than the other two exercises.

Once you have produced these videos and are happy with them, you'll have a nice range of videos for a showreel. You'll also learn what issues you faced, how you could improve the videos next time, and what other kit you could have used. You may want to upload the videos to a site like Vimeo or YouTube so you can easily share them with others.

Summary

In this chapter we have seen why video is an important type of content you should learn about. Video for digital is different from other platforms, so even if you're an experienced video producer you may want to see how you could change your style to better suit digital platforms.

We've also seen why live video is an important type of content to consider making in order to create a conversation with your audience. It is also a powerful tool for events.

You will now have an idea of what equipment you may need to produce the kind of video you want. Video is now something anyone can produce with only a few pieces of equipment; fundamentally, a smartphone is something you can use right away.

While producing video can seem daunting at first, the only way you can learn is by practising. So get your hands on whatever kit you can and begin filming. You will very quickly start improving, setting you up for a career in digital content.

In Chapter 4 we will look at other kinds of content you can produce, from stunning photos to compelling podcasts.

Graphic design, 04 photography and audio

- Improving your other content skills makes you more employable.
- Audio is often overlooked but very important.
- Still imagery can be easier to produce than video.

By following this book you should now have an understanding of effective video and written content. To become multi-skilled, these are just a few of the tools available to you. Powerful photography, audio storytelling and smart graphic design complete the package. By mastering this range of skills you can tell stories on digital any way you like (often mixing formats).

Photography

It would be very hard to find a smartphone without a high-powered camera built into it. While photography was made a lot more accessible with the rise of digital cameras, it was the popularity of smartphones that meant more people than ever before could take high-quality images.

Websites and social networks that let people show off their images also grew in popularity alongside smartphone use (Instagram being the most well-known example). The old saying that a picture is worth a thousand words is true with digital platforms where your audiences' attention is at a premium.

Whether it's taking photos with an old film camera or a phone, the principles of good photography stay the same. By learning these fundamental skills you will be able to take memorable photos that will improve any kind of digital communication. Effective photography is a highly useful skill that you can easily practise.

While video is a very powerful tool for storytelling, it can be more complicated and time-consuming to produce. You usually need more equipment to create video as well. But armed with your smartphone you can take stunning images and send them out to the world instantly.

Dedicated cameras absolutely still have a place in today's digital world. While cameras built into phones are incredibly powerful, they do not have proper lenses. This means that zooming isn't possible on a phone (they have a 'zoom' feature but this is just cropping the photo, meaning it loses quality), whereas cameras can take the highest-quality photos and are more flexible with accessories.

If you want to work in marketing, understanding how photography promotes a brand is important. Having a consistent style and mood in all the images you produce for that brand conveys a message without any words at all. And as we covered in the video section, generally the reading age among adults can be low, so visuals are often needed to get a message across.

The fundamentals of photography

The first rule of photography is: there are no real rules to stunning photos. While there are guidelines and suggestions on taking strong images, ultimately these are not rigid rules to be followed every time. Be as creative as you like. But these guidelines will give you some simple yet powerful techniques to follow that will improve the images you take. Most modern cameras can take care of settings such as exposure and aperture, freeing you up to consider the real fundamentals of photography.

Leading lines

Photos that take you on a visual 'journey' can be really beautiful. Think of a pathway or a road that the eye naturally follows. It doesn't have to be that literal, either. It could be architecture, like a row of windows, or something natural, like the ridges on a crocodile's back, leading away from the viewer.

I took the photo in Figure 4.1 with my phone while on holiday. In a literal way the leading lines take the viewer's eye on a journey down the path into a forest.

4.1

In Figure 4.2 you see the same effect but up close with the subject matter.

4.2

Using leading lines is a simple technique that's worth mastering as it can be used in many different ways.

Rule of thirds

The rule of thirds is possibly the most important technique to learn. When taking a photo it's often natural to frame the person or object exactly in the centre. But this doesn't often look that great.

Whatever the aspect ratio of your picture, imagine a grid dividing it into three rows and three equal columns:

4.3

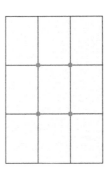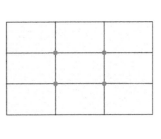

Try positioning the main parts of your photo either along these lines or at the four intersection points. As an example, I composed the photo on the next page using the rule of thirds. You can see how the top of the building on the right follows the gridline at A. And the horizon of the lake follows the line at B.

Helpfully, most photography apps now have a grid that you can simply switch on while you take a photo. You'll quickly find, though, that you won't need it once framing photos in this way becomes natural.

4.4

Symmetry

The human eye is naturally drawn to patterns and symmetry whether it's intentional or not. This can be an easy way to catch people's attention and make your photos look unique.

4.5

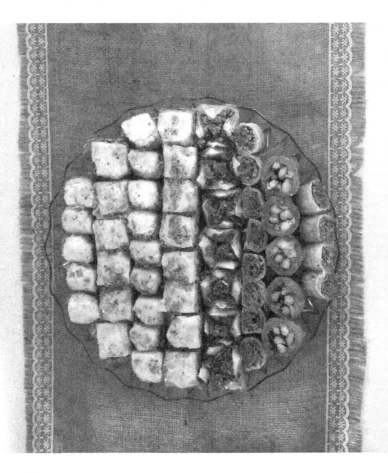

Keep an eye out for naturally occurring symmetry or think about how you can prepare what you want to photograph in a symmetrical way.

Check the background

A shoot can often look great to your eye when you're taking the photos. When you actually see the images, though, the background can often distract from the main subject of the photo. This can often easily be solved by either shooting against a plain backdrop or using a shallow depth of field (where the background is blurred). In this photo taken in Melbourne, the buildings are in contrast to the sky behind them, helping them stand out.

The background doesn't have to be all one colour. I interviewed a man called Peter Snell who runs a nearby bookshop. In this photo you can see him sitting among his books, which helps place the (audio) interview. The slight blur keeps the focus on Peter:

Take your time

This is an easy piece of advice to give but harder to live by. Take your time setting up your equipment and your shot. Don't be afraid to move people around, get into better positions or wait for better light. This can be hard in reality, though, as the situation you're photographing may be moving quickly.

Get close and don't be shy

Try to get as close to your subject as you can. If you're using a smartphone you'll only be losing image quality if you use the built-in zoom feature. Proper zoom lenses can help with this if you are unable to get close to your subject. It's also important to be confident with moving people around. You may feel daft contorting into strange positions to take the perfect shot or barking orders at large groups of people, but ultimately you want the best photo you can take. If you're taking photos of people, talking and joking with them can also help relax them and make the photos look more natural.

Overshoot

Often you will only get one chance to take photos of your subject. Even when it's something you know you can return to, it's best to take as many photos as you can. The days of film with only 32 shots on are long gone. You want to give yourself as many options as possible, and often the spontaneous photos you didn't plan will look the best.

Equipment

There is a vast amount of equipment available to keen photographers. A tripod is essential for taking steady photos and you'll need a flash for photographing in the dark. But how do you know which camera to buy?

- *Smartphones* can take high-quality photos, allow you to share them quickly to social media, and usually have a built-in flash too. They also have the advantage of being commonplace and needing very little training to use. This can be helpful if you're building a team of digital content producers. They are easily the fastest solution available.

Smartphones have two big drawbacks. The first is that they have no proper zoom function. Second, they have limited battery life. If you're using the phone for other features such as video or publishing to social media, you can quickly deplete the battery. Without a backup or a battery booster your 'camera' will be useless.

- *Bridge cameras* are designed to be simple entry-level cameras that let you do lots of things fairly well rather than specializing. You can't change the lens but you get a versatile, zoomable lens and a dedicated camera. They are also much cheaper than a professional DSLR camera.

  Bridge cameras allow you to take professional photos with a dedicated piece of equipment for a low price. They can often be useful as backup cameras too. Naturally, though, the lower cost means they are not as flexible or as powerful as dedicated professional cameras.

- *DSLR (digital single lens reflex) cameras* are professional-standard cameras that allow maximum flexibility and quality. You can change the lens, use professional accessories and shoot stunning video too.

  They require a lot of training to use properly and are expensive, even before you factor in the cost of accessories such as different lenses.

CASE STUDY Murray Close, photographer

Murray Close is an award-winning and internationally renowned photographer whose work hangs in galleries and private collections worldwide. He specializes in on-set film photography and has worked on a huge number of films, including Withnail & I, Jurassic Park, *the Harry Potter and Hunger Games series, and* Mission: Impossible.

I spoke to him about how digital photography has changed his work and the wider industry as well as getting advice for budding photographers.

I got started 35 years ago working with Stanley Kubrick and Warner Bros. The first project I shot on digital in its entirety was *Harry Potter and the Goblet of Fire*. The studios at that point were reluctant to change to digital from film because no one really understood it; they were really obsessed with 'the original'. It was very hard to explain to them that there is no original; you can make as many 'originals' as you want to make with digital. What helped convince them was that working in digital gave a better result, especially in low light situations (a common situation on a film set). So on *The Goblet of Fire* we set up a digital lab on the set and did everything ourselves. Even though this was only about ten years ago, it seems incredibly old-fashioned. It would be much simpler now – it's extraordinary how digital has made everything so much easier.

Now you can't shoot on film anymore – it's just too expensive. There's never been anything wrong with film – I still shoot the odd roll of film just for fun, but when digital came in, that was the end of the classic photography lab.

The rise of digital post-production along with photography isn't a crutch – anything you can use as a tool or that helps you get out of trouble is a good thing. You could say shooting a Polaroid is a crutch too. What post-production has done is increased the photographer's workload immensely, because you're the lab too. I use Lightroom to grade and fix everything I shoot. I'm not contractually required to do it, but it gives me the opportunity to give the clients images that look exactly how they should look. It's not about how I think they should look, but working with the Director of Photography to make sure the images fit the narrative of the project.

Anyone coming out of photography school now will have a strong background in post-production skills. You need to be able to do this along with photography itself. You don't need to be the best Photoshop artist (I'm terrible at it, and was always a bad black-and-white photo printer too), but it's an essential skill for anyone starting out. I do find that the photographers who are fantastic at post-production spend too much time in front of their computer, though.

Getting started in photography has actually become more expensive over the years. You now need a powerful laptop and probably a home computer too to render your files. When I got started you just needed a few cameras, a light meter, four lenses and a bag. Now, you need a lot more kit.

Any photographer will use their smartphone and can get great images on it. One of my pet peeves is seeing people in a touristy place taking pointless photographs on their smartphones. You can maybe use yours to learn the basics of composition, but if you're serious about your photography you have to learn the fundamentals. If anything, you learn by finding out where you went wrong. I tell people to never even use the automatic settings on their cameras.

I have to keep my website up to date because I don't have a paper portfolio. It has to look slick and work well, and it's something photographers have to invest their money in. Your site is your marketplace and calling card. Sites like Flickr or Instagram can be good to sell your material, but you might not get lots of work from them.

Once I shot *Sense8* I had a deluge of Instagram followers who are rabid fans of the show. Social media channels are really important to the movie studios. Before, they would hold on to my photos for as long as possible to try to keep it a secret. Now, it's a different world. *Sense8* would release five or ten images from the set frequently, just to keep people interested. If you're trying to sell or market a product, these channels are terrific. They get people speaking about the show and create a buzz. We also have influencers, who have large audiences on social media channels, visiting a lot of TV programme sets and films to help promote them.

If you want to get into professional photography, the markets are very different. The disciplines of sports photography are totally different from fashion, for example. It's very important to get good training because there are so many technical skills to understand. You can teach yourself , though – there are lots of very good online courses. It's great to get some tips from people who know what you're trying to achieve. You might be trying to do something specific, and having someone who can say 'Here's a trick, here's how you do that' can save you so much time.

I've always been of the mind that you're not shooting for your own portfolio but for the client. You have to be aware of the market. For Harry Potter I might be photographing something that could be turned into a toy. You wouldn't be doing that for a Scorsese film.

Exercise

For this exercise, take a series of photos using a mix of the techniques listed before. It doesn't matter what you use to take them – a smartphone will be absolutely fine. Decide on what mood or story you want to convey in the images as well, as that may change how you take the photos.

It's then worth posting them to a photography community like Flickr or Instagram and asking for feedback. You can also analyse other people's photos as well. Choose ten photos that you love and try to establish why you like them so much. Do they follow any of the rules listed earlier? Is there a technique or style you can try yourself?

Once you have equipment you can practise photography virtually anywhere and very quickly build up your skills. It's not only a valuable skill to have for potential employers but is also accessible and, most importantly, a lot of fun.

Audio

Despite the invention of television, the internet and smartphones, radio and audio have still remained popular. When thinking about digital, audio is often overshadowed by other types of content such as video and graphic design. Sometimes the reason for this is commercial – video advertising rates pay best. But audio has a big advantage over other kinds of content – you can enjoy it while doing other things. Until driverless cars come along, there's no way you'll be able to (safely) watch video or read an article while you're driving. Podcasts that you can download and listen to at any time have also continued rising in popularity since their launch, especially with the release of shows like *Serial*.

Social media networks are also waking up to the importance of audio. Facebook announced Live Audio to complement their Live Video tool at the end of 2016. Spotify has sharing features built in and sites like Soundcloud specialize in audio sharing.

Audio often lets you tell an in-depth story better than with video. People tend to tune in for longer than with video too, as they are often making an 'appointment to view' – ie choosing specifically to listen to your podcast or broadcast at a time that suits them. You may want to discuss a subject that is hard to represent visually, such as economics or a historical event.

Audio is often easier to capture too. If you want to interview people, camera kits and video can feel intimidating. If you're just recording audio on a smartphone, your subjects are likely to be a lot more relaxed and will open up. It's easier to produce, as obviously you don't need to worry about visuals and you need a lot less equipment.

While you need less equipment to produce audio, there is, of course, still an awful lot of skill behind creating compelling stories with audio alone. And if you want to pursue a career that specializes in audio, such as at a radio station, you still mustn't neglect your other content creation skills. Producing video will still be a major part of your role and will complement audio storytelling beautifully. You might have some powerful audio with a set of photos taken from the recording too. You could use video editing software to add the photos over the top of the audio, creating a video product.

It works the other way round too – understanding what makes great audio will complement your video production. If you want to specialize in writing, understanding the power of audio opens many opportunities for you to combine sound with your creative content.

Fundamental skills

If you want to specialize in audio, what are the main skills you need? Producing audio for digital platforms is very different from live radio broadcasting where you would need to understand mixing desks, broadcasting laws and more. Clearly this book will focus just on digital audio production.

Depending on the career you go on to have, you may be quickly recording audio soundbites from a news story, recording full-length programmes or producing from events. You may also need to quickly go live on to social media. Here are some fundamental skills that you should practise that will be useful in any of the situations where you may need to record audio.

Interview technique

Most audio content involves you speaking to someone else. You might naturally be good at having conversations or a painfully shy introvert – either way it's important not to treat an interview like a normal conversation:

- Have in mind what you want to get out of the interview. Work out beforehand what you're going to ask and what the person is likely to say. Think of a roadmap – you can take plenty of different routes but you want to end up at your destination. Your conversation and questions shouldn't be written in stone, but you want to make sure you end the interview where you want it.

- When interviewing someone, remember the Five Ws – what happened, who was involved, where was it, when did it happen, and why? These questions give you the basic foundation of any story.

- Don't over-ask questions. You may have only a few minutes to speak to someone and you don't want to spend that time speaking over them or not giving them the space to answer properly. You'll also need to learn when to cut people off or prompt them, but remember they should be doing most of the speaking.

- Listen to the answer. It can be nerve-racking when you're recording a big interview and you may be thinking about what to ask next. But you don't want to accidentally ask a question that's already been answered. Pay attention to what the person is saying and use that to inform what question you ask next rather than being too prescriptive.

- Pay attention to where you're recording. If you're at a football match you will have the sound of the crowd or music in the background. This can add nice detail to the interview, but if you're standing right by a speaker it will make the audio unusable. Have the confidence to ask someone to step into a different room or location if they are not clear on the audio. Sometimes this won't be as obvious as a large speaker – someone could be nervously tapping a pen or a loud air conditioner in the background could be humming away.

Storytelling

Because audio is very intimate and accessible it's a fantastic medium on which to tell powerful stories. Pre-recorded audio and live audio have very different ways of interesting the listener, though.

With pre-recorded audio shared as a podcast or on an audio site it's likely your listener is making an intentional choice to listen. This means they will have more patience and you need to gradually reveal the story to keep them interested.

Follow a clear narrative arc that explains the story over a few minutes or an hour – gradually reveal more as the programme goes on. If it's an advert or a promo, clearly you have a very small amount of time to get your message across. While an hour-long documentary programme gives you lots of space to tell your story, it is also a rare skill to keep the listener engaged over this period of time.

For live audio it's the reverse – you need an exciting hook at the beginning to capture the audience's attention. Plant an idea in your listener's minds that's exciting and makes them want to find out more about what's coming up. This could be a tease, or posing a question to the audience to think about. It's much the same as with social media video. You have to capture the audience's attention very quickly as they have so much content available to them.

Because you are not using a visual medium, you must use language to paint a picture in the listener's mind. Like good creative writing, you will need to practise this. As a short exercise, get used to quickly describing the situations around you and see if they make sense to people who aren't there.

Ultimately you want to surprise the listener. They want to learn about something they never knew before, or feel moved by the story you are telling. This goes back to the roadmap metaphor. Think about what journey you want to take the listener on and where you want to end up.

Finally, you need to find and develop your own voice. By having a unique way of telling stories you will create something that stands out and helps you build a personal brand. Have the confidence to be yourself. Having an individual voice is especially important with audio where your audience can only listen to you.

Using sound effectively

Speech is just one part of the story when creating audio content. You need sound and possibly music to create truly compelling material. Some of this will be as simple as what the place you're recording in sounds like. If you're recording an interview at a football match, you want to capture some of the atmosphere.

It's easy to assume the listener knows where you are, though. You must explain any sound quickly in an audio piece as it may confuse the listener. Let's take the football match example again – if you start with the roar of the crowd and then a sports star whom you're interviewing starts speaking, the listener won't know where you are, especially if they don't know who the footballer is. Use sound to help you tell a story but make sure you explain what's going on.

For pre-recorded content, remember to capture what's known as 'wild track' when you are producing audio in a location. This is a minute or so of the general background noise with no voice whatsoever. This is useful for a couple of reasons:

- When you come to edit the audio piece, you have plenty of background sound to add where you need it.

- It's likely your interviews will need some editing. This could be as simple as removing long pauses, errors or second takes. Without wild track the listener will hear a sudden jump cut. With wild track you have that constant background noise to mask any cuts. Obviously, it's important to uphold editorial values and not misinterpret what someone's saying when doing this.

A final piece of advice for any pre-recorded audio content you produce – don't interfere with the 'master' recordings. Don't do any editing on the move unless you absolutely have to. Back up the original, unedited audio as soon as you can and then start editing once you've made a copy. Without doing this, you might make a mistake which you are then stuck with, as you have edited the only file you have.

Live audio

Content that's live offers an obvious immediacy and authenticity to the listener. Just as with any kind of live broadcast, the risks are also greater. Tools like Facebook Live Audio allow your audience to interact, much like a classic radio phone-in. Because of this, broadcasting live audio can feel more complex as you have to be aware of many things going on at the same time – the interview itself, the audience reaction or your equipment.

Often the key to success with live broadcast is preparation. Here are some things to consider when planning a live audio broadcast:

- *Questions*. Have you done your research and are you confident about what you're going to ask? Have you thought about what the likely answers are going to be and how you'll respond?

- *People*. Is everyone you need to speak to available at the right time? If you're speaking to multiple guests one after the other, have you got someone to help keep track of time and handle them?

- *Kit*. Are your battery levels okay? Do you have all the equipment you'll need easily to hand? Do you have backups for the most important pieces of equipment?

- *Surroundings*. Is there any loud background noise that may interrupt your broadcast? Do you have enough space to move around if you need to? Never underestimate how disruptive the public can be.

- *Interacting with the audience*. Are you able to keep track of the comments coming in from listeners? Is your interviewee aware that your followers will be asking questions too?

- *Backup*. Have a plan B. If you have promoted the live broadcast extensively, think about what could go wrong and what you can do to mitigate it.

Equipment

There is a lot less equipment needed to start producing audio compared to video content. There are also lots of free audio editing apps too, so you don't need to purchase any expensive software. And as with video, a smartphone is an incredibly powerful way to start producing audio.

Here are some suggested pieces of kit you could invest in to get started:

- *Smartphone* – you can record fantastic quality audio from your smartphone. The built-in microphones are excellent quality and you have the advantage of having the phone with you at all times. You can also use it to broadcast directly to social media.

    You can also set it to back up any audio recordings you make to the cloud, automatically, giving you some extra security. There are also plenty of great apps that let you quickly edit material straight from your phone, although detailed editing should be done on a desktop.

    Any sort of recording done on a phone does drain the battery quickly, so a battery booster may be useful.

- *Smartphone microphone* – while the built-in microphones on smartphones are very good quality, you may want something more serious. There are plenty of microphones on the market designed for your model of phone, some of which have long cables which are very useful when interviewing somebody.

- *Solid state recorder* – if you want a dedicated device that captures better-quality audio, invest in a solid state voice recorder. These have enormous capacity and decent battery life as well as professional-quality microphones. They are cheaper than buying a smartphone just for audio and give you something a lot more powerful to use.

- *Software* – unless you're broadcasting live audio, you will need to edit the material you've recorded. Thankfully, there are a number of free editing apps out there, such as Audacity, that are very powerful and allow you to build up your skills. By learning to use this software you'll easily be able to transition into commercial software used by professional producers.

Exercise

You'll need to build up your experience in telling a story or explaining a situation to an audience that can't see what you can. This exercise is designed to test these skills but is also a useful way to build up your public-speaking skills in general.

Choose an event or location and visit with a way of recording your voice – this could just be your smartphone.

When you get there, spend the day describing the event through recorded audio. Practise with recordings of different lengths – how would you describe what's going on in 30 seconds compared to 10 minutes?

Once you have completed your recordings, ask someone who wasn't with you to listen to them and get their feedback. Did they have a clear idea of what was going on? And if so, did you make it sound compelling?

You can then review these recordings and think about what you would do differently or what you could do in the edit to improve the quality of the pieces.

CASE STUDY Jonathan Harper, designer

Jon Harper is an experienced designer who has worked for clients such as Jack Daniels, The Guardian, Shell and Timberland. We spoke about his career and some of the lessons he's learnt along the way.

I studied Graphic Design and Communications and when I left I had no idea how creative agencies were structured or how they worked. I had no understanding of how the different departments collaborated or the relationship between account management, the project managers, the strategists and the art workers, so my early career was quite the learning experience.

After graduating I was very fortunate to have some work exhibited at the D&AD New Blood awards, where a senior art director at the advertising agency Ogilvy saw it and asked me to come in for a chat. We got on well and I was offered a two-week placement. Luckily that turned into six months – an overwhelming six months because I ended up doing more work during that time than I'd done in the previous two years.

After the placement was over, I wanted to do something a bit more creative, which perhaps was ego driven. I lacked perspective on how valuable the experience at Ogilvy had been. It taught me a valuable lesson: if you're junior in this industry, get one whole year under your belt at an agency. It changes your future employers' perception of you because you have such a recognizable brand name on your CV.

I then worked at a number of different creative agencies, did some freelance work, did some more placements and generally took whatever opportunity I could get. Finally, I landed a job at an agency where I spent four years. I was so fortunate to join a team of senior designers who mentored and taught me every day. I worked with people who really wanted to develop my career and gave me fantastic design opportunities. The team worked so hard but it was worth it. I became the brand guardian on an American whiskey brand, which was very fulfilling.

In this role, I learnt to listen to people. I learnt the value of being in a team, rather than of always seeing yourself as the best designer. I was also very fortunate to get the opportunity to mentor juniors and push their talents. The team were close – it felt telepathic.

When I decided to leave, it was because I got offered more money. Huge mistake. I'd been like a cartoon character with the $ signs in his eyes and, inevitably, I was unhappy in the new role. I left after six months to join a team that I knew for certain I'd get on well with and who'd push my career. I now work at an agency where I get on with my bosses and I can be creative.

Throughout this journey, I was always thinking about my portfolio. A great portfolio was always my goal. Obviously it's nice to be part of a good company, but I had to think about my portfolio and what creative opportunities I could find to keep improving it. In my own time I would design fonts or gig posters, I'd do tutorials and experiment with graphic treatments or corporate identities for start-ups. If you're on a project you don't like, you sometimes get these personal creative ideas that you can't get out of your head until you make them. Three of these have actually been the biggest boosts to my career in terms of getting noticed.

If you're just starting out as a designer, you won't yet have a personal brand or full professional portfolio, which is why these extra creative activities are so important. We've picked junior designers because of their personal projects and their drive. We had a junior who was just 17 come in to the agency. He didn't have a degree because he couldn't afford the university fees, but his work was so good and he was so determined that we took him on. He's still at the agency four years later. Drive and talent are the most important things: some of the best designers I know went to university, and some of them didn't.

You can have days where you feel absolutely invincible. But then you have days where you just can't crack a brief, or you see the work from someone totally new that makes you reassess everything. Sometimes working in this field can be challenging, when you're not allowed to be creative or you get negative feedback. The client may know exactly what they want, and you can't take it personally. It's hard, but ultimately they're paying for the work.

I've never found designing for digital drastically different from print in terms of principles. Ultimately it's about the idea and the clarity of the communication. You've got to keep it simple. If you're producing a lot of content, make sure there's a discipline across all the images. Is the typography treated consistently? Is the positioning of the assets consistent?

The most common mistake I see is a lack of attention to detail. It's quite common that I see design portfolios that are full of spelling errors. I hate that. When it comes to design, typesetting is so important – your choice of fonts is important. Think about the tone of voice. Check the kerning, positioning and so on. You don't want these things clashing. And make notes – I can't stress enough how important that is. You don't want to miss a bit of feedback or an idea, tip or suggestion.

It can be a competitive industry, and one of the negative things about it is that it can be elitist (another part of the reason I was so keen for that 17-year-old to get the job). If you put your work on the internet, or on Instagram, that's a huge opportunity. I didn't have that option ten years ago. Social media means you can get people to see your work every day. There are so many channels out there to help you get your work seen. Opportunity is everything, and it's like that poster – work hard and be nice to people.

Make friends. Listen to people. Ask yourself if that's the best you can do. Enjoy it.

Graphic design

While a picture may be worth a thousand words, you'll often need to explain something in more detail. By adding text and information to photos, you can create compelling content that quickly conveys a lot of information without the need to produce a video. Graphic design is something you can specialize in, but by learning some simple techniques and tools you can create smart-looking images.

Understanding graphic design isn't just about messaging, though. The mood conveyed by typography, colour and style is an important part of communications and branding. Thankfully, you don't need expensive equipment to design content, and the software you can use is getting easier to use.

Let's look at some intentionally bad examples that show how colour, font and layout can affect both the message and mood conveyed by your image.

First, here's a photo of Westminster Abbey.

4.8

Now, if the authorities in charge of London tourism used this image to encourage people to visit, it would be a disaster. The murky, foggy photo combined with the gothic font and dark colours makes London look like a very depressing place to take a holiday.

Let's now do the reverse.

4.9

Nobody likes paying more taxes. So using a sunny photo, a childish font and a cheap-looking text-warp effect would be a terrible way to let people know.

These examples may seem flippant, but poor design is a common problem. I once received a letter from my doctor about a serious medical matter written in Comic Sans.

When designing for digital platforms, having clear, effective design is important for a number of reasons:

- In a busy social media feed, your content needs to look distinctive and pleasing to the eye so that it stands out.

- As most people will see the content on a smartphone (obviously a much smaller canvas than a television or a poster) where space is at a premium, you have to know how to design for a smaller screen.

- It makes your brand, story or message consistently recognizable. Famous logos like the Nike tick or Apple apple don't have the company names in them, but most people recognize them instantly.

There is a huge community of graphic designers online, with people sharing tips and tricks. You'll quickly be able to find guides on any graphic design style or technique you want to try out.

Some fundamentals of design

Colour

Colour theory is a complex subject, but thankfully there are some main principles you should keep in mind.

First, the colours used affect the mood of the image. For example, red evokes passionate feelings such as love or anger. Blue creates a calm, cool look. Green is often used to convey nature or environmental themes.

The colours you use can have multiple meanings depending on the other design elements. If you use an aggressive font coloured red, you will create an angry, aggressive mood. Switch it to a cursive font and it instantly becomes romantic. Think carefully about what colour palette you're going to use, especially if you're creating a visual brand for the first time. What do the colours convey?

Also remember that some of your audience will be colour blind. They can find it especially hard to distinguish reds and greens from one another. If you're using colours to help people distinguish elements, for example on a road map, keep in mind that some of your audience will be colour blind, so consider designing in a different way. For example, you may combine the colour with patterns too.

The colour wheel is an important part of design that also easily helps you choose complementary colours. Any design app will have a colour wheel within it, or you can just use a search engine and save one.

A simple way to discover which colours complement one another is to see what's on the opposite side of the colour wheel. When thinking about what colours you want to use, simply choose a primary colour and see what's on the other side of the colour wheel.

Think about the shades of colour you want to use as well. Vibrant, intense primary colours are attention-grabbing and bold. Neutral or pastel colours look calming and subtle.

Typography

Deciding what typeface or font to use can be a hard decision. You can be spoilt for choice, with thousands of beautiful and unique typefaces to choose from. These are just as central to conveying mood as colour.

The most obvious factor to consider is how the font looks. Is it appropriate to the style you want to convey?

If the content you're designing is storytelling or journalistic, you will want a clean, simple font that doesn't distract from the writing. If you're creating a lifestyle brand, you will want a font that's lively, creative and interesting, to reflect the product you're selling.

Once you have chosen a font, think about whether it's appropriate in all the situations you want to use it in (the Comic Sans example from earlier is an example of getting this wrong). You may want a bold and distinctive font for your logo, but that same font may get extremely tiring if you use it for all the text on your content. Do some research into the font as well. Take the 'Visit London' image on page 91. The person who chole it may have thought it looked 'medieval' or 'typical early English' or 'authentically old', or even simply 'British'. But it is none of these.

Experiment with your chosen font in a number of different settings and check it looks good in all of them.

Clean, simple sans serif typefaces are often popular for their simple and modern look. Despite this, don't be afraid to choose a loud and heavily designed typeface – just use it in moderation.

It's important to check the readability of your typeface too. The style and mood of the typeface should always be secondary to how clear it is. It can be tempting to pick highly stylized designs, but check they work well in small sizes or in lighter shades.

Lines and placement

Lines are likely to appear in your designs in one form or another. Straight lines, be they literal lines or square shapes, look formal, serious or corporate. Thick, hand-drawn or curved lines can look playful and creative.

You can also make text follow lines as well. It can be as simple as following a slight curve or a more random design.

It's worth experimenting with how different lines can change the feel of an image. Here's a pretend logo for a mixing studio. Both use straight lines but you can see they feel quite different.

4.10

Space

Good design is as much about what you leave out. Images can often look cluttered or busy. Not only does this look bad, it confuses the message you want to get across. The trend towards leaving a lot of white space in a design is especially popular in web design where clean, clear design is favoured.

Complex, busy design can look distinctive and vibrant, but it's very hard to get right. Using too much space can make an image look too small or unfinished, but generally leave plenty of room for the elements to breathe. The next example from our pretend mixing studio has a very basic, clean design.

4.11

Modal Mixing Studio

Brand world

You may have heard of brand or style guidelines before. These are instructions used by brands and organizations to ensure their content looks consistent. They provide clear guidance on what typeface to use, what colour palette to use and how elements should be placed together. They usually also include tone-of-voice guidance for written content.

These have plenty of advantages and you should consider creating at the very least a simple set of guidelines. Even if it's just for yourself, brand guidelines can help you keep your content looking consistent. It also means that if you ever have anyone else producing content for you, they can adhere to your style.

Creating a brand guidelines document can also be a useful creative exercise as it forces you to think carefully about how your designed content will look.

Brand guides do have drawbacks, though. In a multiplatform world a beautifully designed logo may look wonderful on stationery or a poster, but it may not work on social media. If you worked for an airline you'd have to consider how the branding would look both on the side of a plane and on a business card. It can therefore be very hard to capture all possible uses of your design in a brand guidelines document.

More designers are instead thinking of 'brand worlds'. They create a look and feel for a brand that can easily be used in a number of situations, rather than providing highly prescriptive advice.

If you want to make a brand guidelines document, here's what you should include:

- the logo itself, showing how it can be used, how it should be sized according to other elements, and how it shouldn't be used;

- typography, showing what typefaces should be used and how they relate to one another;

- the colours your brand uses, along with technical details so designers can quickly work with them (the hex codes used by designers would be useful);

- real-life examples showing how the designs should be used.

Exercise

Imagine someone has come to you to design elements for their new business – a café. Use design software or sketch how you would design smart-looking logos for their business.

They have told you they want the café to appeal to a wealthy, upmarket crowd. Think about how this will influence the content you design for them.

Now imagine they have contacted you with news of a dramatic U-turn – the café is now a child-friendly play centre where kids get to pretend to be baristas.

How would you change the content you've designed to appeal to this completely different audience?

As with the photography exercise, it is worth sharing your work with design communities online and asking for feedback. Video-sharing sites like YouTube are a fantastic place to learn new techniques which, combined with feedback from online communities, will get you off to a great start.

Summary

In this chapter we have looked at how to produce different kinds of content. Any digital creative needs at least a basic grasp of how to produce each kind of content. The most memorable pieces often combine powerful photography with writing and audio elements too. By being able to produce different kinds of content you will have a powerful toolchest of storytelling methods available to you, and you'll need these skills for most digital creative jobs out there.

So far we have focused on the production of content. But once you've mastered making the stuff, how do you build an audience to share it with?

Digital community building

05

- It's essential to speak with your community. Don't just broadcast at them.
- Set the rules of engagement.
- Keep trying new things to keep your audience interested.

When social media first became popular it was often used simply to broadcast. Organizations thought they could succeed by just endlessly publishing stuff to this exciting new platform and their job was done. The problem was that, despite getting plenty of video views and web clicks, the size of their audiences often wasn't growing. The clue with social media is in the name – it's a social platform where people talk.

The organizations that have grown the fastest are the ones who actively communicate with their audiences – so not just publishing a video but responding quickly to questions and queries in the comments, and not just writing pieces but asking people what their views are on important issues and using that to inform their writing. It's about making people feel valued and invested in what you're trying to do.

Building an active community is essential for any commercial strategy too. If you are a news publisher, you need people to pay to read your journalism. In an enormously competitive world you have to make them want to fund your work. You can only do this if they feel supportive of your work and that they have a share in it. If your publishing strategy is based on volume (for example, getting as many video views/web clicks as possible), you have to build as large an audience as possible.

If you want to promote your business or product, having followers who will actively promote you is more powerful than any kind of advertising. You'll also be able to spot problems quickly by seeing what your customers are saying. People may have valid complaints, but with the right approach and a positive community you can turn an angry customer into a happy advocate.

An active community doesn't just apply to commercial organizations. If you are promoting a cause or an important message, that will be amplified by your audience – if they are engaged and care about what you're doing.

Up to this point we have covered the practicalities of making content for digital. For it to be of any use, you need to have an audience to actually *see* it. Building a loyal and engaged audience is a real sign of success when it comes to producing content. Fundamentally, it shows that your content is interesting to people. But building a community is about more than that – it's having people who will share your content to new audiences, who will discuss and debate the message you're trying to send, and who will ultimately fund your work.

You may find yourself working for a brand that already has a large community – a famous newspaper or product, for example. This does make your life easier in some ways as you don't have to go through the slog of building an audience from scratch. On the other hand, that community expects certain things from your organization, and if you don't understand them you can annoy the very people who follow your work. By keeping up to date with ways of keeping your community active and engaged, you can help make sure you've got an audience ready to view and share the content you make.

Large organizations frequently struggle with the need to sound friendly and human on social media while also having strict policies and guidelines. If everyone managing their digital channels understands what works well with their audiences, this becomes easier. Admittedly, this can be easier said than done, but with some trial and error, evaluation and common sense an organization can quickly establish what their audience really likes.

Building a community

There are three main rules for building an active and interested audience.

Be human

As we covered in the section on plain English, it is often too easy to lapse into corporate speak and jargon. People want to feel that they are speaking to other people rather than faceless organizations. If they have questions or views they want to share them and receive a response. If you can make your audience laugh, feel valued or passionate about a cause, they will remain loyal. You can only do this by being human and approachable. If you're dealing with complaints, often even completely irate people will calm down rapidly if they feel they are speaking to real people rather than organizations.

In practical terms, this means thinking carefully about your organization's tone of voice, making sure that any overly formal or pompous language is avoided and that you are as personable as possible with people on social media. This can be a huge challenge to get right in large organizations. It's easy to go too far and sound inappropriately casual when there is a very serious problem. If a customer has a minor complaint, using emotive and casual language will help calm them down. However, if they have had a serious injury thanks to your company, they will not be impressed by relaxed-sounding social media messages. You can only find the sweet spot through trial and error, as every organization and brand will be different.

Be interesting

It's easy just to churn out content while giving little thought to whether people would actually be interested in the material. Sure, a video may contain all your organization's messaging, be slickly produced and make your boss happy, but if it falls flat with your audience, what good has it done?

The basis of all good digital content is simple – produce stuff people are interested in. It sounds easy but the reality is much harder. How do you know what your audience likes? And once you know that, what barriers are there internally to stop you making it? You might even find that you don't have the kit or skills to produce it.

You can overcome this through a combination of science and art. By keeping a close eye on your digital analytics you'll quickly be able to establish what works well with your audience. What are they most engaged with? What subjects do they comment on the most? What sorts of content are they most likely to share with their friends? You will be successful if you frequently check your analytics and rapidly change your approach when necessary.

You still need to trust your gut, though. You'll need to plan imaginative and creative new content ideas. Once you've built a community you'll soon develop a sixth sense for what will work well with them. Again, this is another situation where you will learn through trial and error. Look for an emotional hook in all the content you produce – it could make people laugh, feel passionate, find the content useful and informative, want to share it with their friends, or even make them feel angry. The worst outcome is that people feel indifferent towards your content.

Be listening

These rules are simple but can often be hard to follow, especially in larger organizations. Just getting really effective content right is hard enough. People expect to interact with organizations on social media instantly and have their opinions heard. It might sound entitled but in an era of instant communications, why should it be any different for your organization?

Your audience must feel valued and that their opinion matters to you. This is important for you too – by listening to your audience you learn what's working and what's not. It can be galling when you put a lot of effort into a new type of content only for it to annoy your audience in unexpected ways. But this is much better than ignoring them and continuing to publish material they don't like. People would start unfollowing you, your audience would shrink and your brand would be damaged.

Think carefully about what people get out of following you. It can be as simple as 'they want to be entertained' or something more formal, such as finding out important business information. Keeping in mind what your audience wants from your content helps keep your content relevant and interesting.

In practical terms, how do you listen to your audience effectively?

CASE STUDY Mumsnet CEO Justine Roberts

Justine Roberts is the CEO of Mumsnet, an online community she founded in 2000. It has rapidly grown to a site with 10 million monthly uniques as well as hosting interviews with prime ministers and celebrities. I spoke to her about building and managing a community.

The idea for Mumsnet came about after a disastrous first family holiday with my children. We went to a terrible resort and there were a lot of parents bemoaning how bad it was. It made me think it would be useful to have somewhere not just for parents to suggest and review holiday destinations but to discuss all the other stuff that comes with being a parent. The internet seemed to be a perfect place to tap into that wisdom. We tried to raise some money but then the dotcom crash happened – the gold rush was over and we couldn't raise any.

Our business plan was worthless but it was ultimately a good thing. We had planned to base it around e-commerce that never happened, we didn't have a swanky office or a burn rate, but instead grew it organically. It started to take on a life on its own as it became obvious how useful it was to people. By focusing on the users rather than worrying about making a quick buck it's become an authentic, trusted brand. When we surveyed our users we found the vast majority bought things recommended on the site by other users because it's a trusted environment.

Fast forward to nearer history with the 2010 UK election – sometimes labelled the 'Mumsnet election' – where politicians and senior leaders were queuing up to hold web chats with our users. We realized we had the attention of politicians and felt it would be remiss not to campaign on behalf of our users for the issues they cared about, such as miscarriage care, retailers not sexualizing young girls, or parents with children with special needs.

Community management and social media marketing skills are in huge demand – they are hard to find. If you want to build a community, you've got to think of the user as the most important person in the room. You have to be prepared to listen and engage with them. It's easier at first, but when the community grows, this becomes harder. You have to commit to a spirit of democracy. And you certainly need to be resilient. People can send me aggressive e-mails but then apologize the next day, saying they were having a bad night. You can't take things personally.

With our community we have a lot of debate and work really hard on having diverse opinion. We moderate very much with the view that we may not agree with what you're saying but we'll support your right to say it – as long as you're civilized! Mumsnet is for all parents, not just a particular type of parent. We try to let the conversation flow and keep intervention to a minimum. We are very proactive with people who try to shut down debate – that's against the rules. It's one of the trickiest areas of community management, and people can be passionate about subjects to the point of being unreasonable. The hardest thing is trying to protect the minority view against the majority view. We have a goal to prevent 'aggressive orthodoxies' prevailing over parts of our site.

An example came up in a forum on our site for dog owners. A group of people became the loudest voices on there; they were aggressive about their view that people should only get dogs from rescue centres. I remember a poor woman posting about how she bought a puppy but her husband had since died of cancer. She didn't know what to do and posted for help. The immediate reaction was 'Hmm, but you didn't get the dog from a rescue centre?' We stepped in and said that wasn't acceptable, which was hard because technically no one was breaking the rules. But when an orthodoxy that prevents a contrary point of view takes hold, that's when we step in. Our users feel that the site's theirs, so it's very hard.

We intentionally don't mark or respect how long people have been members of the site. We want everyone to feel welcome, regardless of whether they are completely new or have been a member for years. It also helps stop things becoming stale.

The great thing about Mumsnet is the daily acts of kindness I see. In a world when we are all busy and the internet is presented as a vicious den of trolls, Mumsnet shows that it isn't all like that. People go out of their way to help complete strangers. For example, a lady went on holiday with her family and got to the airport realizing she had left her child's favourite toy behind. She posted on the forum and someone actually turned up at the airport with the same toy and gave it to her. That's kindness in a very physical sense, but virtually we see people going out of their way to help others all the time too; supporting people with breastfeeding issues in the middle of the night or shepherding someone through leaving their abusive husband.

Finding out what they think

Listening to your audience properly is one of those things that's easier said than done. It's certainly easier if you're running a brand by yourself or managing a small team. How do large organizations cope? It's easy to feel swamped on social media if vast numbers of people are messaging you or sharing your content. Here are some techniques you can use to help learn and monitor what your audience wants.

Comments and messages

It's the obvious place to begin – what they are actually saying about your content. Once you share your content, don't assume the job is finished. Keep an eye on the comments, respond to questions and keep speaking to your audience. If they know they can have a conversation with you, they will remain engaged. Don't ignore private messages either, as this is usually most people's first port of call when they have a query. If you're pressed for time you can set up initial automatic responses, but don't let these become a crutch. You must follow up with a proper response once you find the time.

It may also be worth sharing especially positive or interesting messages with your team as a way to boost morale.

Sentiment analysis

Let's say you end up working on a social media brand with an absolutely enormous audience. There's no way you can look at every comment, but you need to find out what your audience thinks about you. This is where sentiment analysis can come in handy. This is special software or evaluation that analyses the words, actions and personality of people discussing words or subjects you set. For example, some very basic sentiment analysis could be around the word cheeseburger. You're likely to see it used in conjunction with words such as delicious, tasty, fast food and unhealthy. No surprises there. Another example could be that your company has just released a new product. If the sentiment analysis shows that people feel very negatively towards this product and the words faulty, broken, confusing and useless keep appearing, you know the company has a serious problem on its hands.

It does have its limits, though. It's expensive, usually requires specialists to set up properly and actually isn't highly accurate. It usually can't spot sarcasm or jokes. For example, it could class the comment 'I just *love* your new product, it's *so much* fun waiting hours for it to work' as a highly positive endorsement.

So it can be useful for broad-brush, big-picture analysis, but don't rely on it too much.

Feedback

Don't be afraid to ask for feedback. You could run surveys, ask people to submit ideas or run large-scale focus groups. Surveys are an easy way to gauge feedback quickly, but keep them as short as possible. It can often be tempting to try to cram as many questions in as possible, but people will quickly get bored. Small, frequent surveys work better than occasional, complex ones. If you do need to run an in-depth survey, it's worth considering offering a prize or incentive of some sort to encourage people to commit to the whole thing.

Crunch the numbers

Data can give you a lot of insight without having to do anything. If the retention rate of your videos is extremely low (this means the percentage of people watching who kept viewing until a certain point), your video simply isn't interesting to your audience. If people leave your website quickly or spend a lot of time searching for pages before leaving, you know it's poorly designed.

Depending on your organization's resources, you may have access to dedicated data analysts. Be clear about what you are trying to find out and what success looks like. You still need to combine rigorous analysis of the data with human intuition, though. For example, a content campaign could have fantastic engagement statistics, but when you look into it this was only because people were commenting to point out an embarrassing typo.

Moderation

Where do you draw the line? It's one of the commonest questions I'm asked when it comes to digital content. Knowing how to manage and moderate your audience's commentary is tricky to get right and different for every organization. If you're managing a political debate show's social profiles, you would have a much higher tolerance for fiery opinion and disagreement than, say, a children's video channel.

The sad but unsurprising truth is that a lot of comments online are unwelcome, ranging from the irrelevant to the outright hateful. Much like responding to audiences, moderating content from your audience can take up an awful lot of time. Thankfully, there are a number of automated solutions out there that can help reduce this burden.

The first step is to create a moderation policy. This gives your team a framework to judge comments by and know when to escalate things. You have to have some tolerance for unhappy comments or disagreement, otherwise your audience won't trust you when they can plainly see that any dissent is just deleted. But knowing what should be deleted makes a lot of people who work in digital content nervous. This is why a moderation policy is so useful. They take many different forms, but the traffic light system is easy to understand and effective.

In the example table, you'll see different types of comment classed as green, yellow or red.

Table 5.1 How to rank comments

Green	Yellow	Red
Positive, supportive comments	Unhappy followers complaining about the content or highlighting errors	Discriminatory and/or abusive language
Insightful debate or challenge	Angry comments without abusive language	Threats against individuals or organizations

(Continued)

Table 5.1   *(Continued)*

Green	Yellow	Red
User-generated content	Unverified complaints about the organization	Spam or fraudulent links
Genuine complaints about the wider organization	People saying they find the content offensive	Exposing confidential information

Once types of comment are classified as green, yellow or red, you can then lay out how they should be responded to. For example:

Green Respond publicly, share their thoughts in your content, pass on useful information internally.

Yellow Continue to monitor the comments, verify complaints to see if they are valid, establish whether the content is correct.

Red Escalate internally, to the social networks or to the authorities. Delete comments and ban users.

By creating and sharing a policy with your team you provide clarity and guidance in a fast-moving world. These policies can work wonderfully with automated filtering. Most social networks allow you to create banned phrase lists to delete swear words automatically. You can also get more advanced paid-for services that let you prevent severe comments from ever being posted.

Going live

The most authentic and often most effective way of interacting with your community is by going live. This could be a written Q&A session, a live video or an audio broadcast. Live video especially has grown in popularity over the past few years as it has become easier to produce. The BBC often hosts live video discussions with its journalists to explain complex news stories. Organizations with specific recruitment needs often host Q&A sessions with current employees to give prospective staff members guidance on what working there is really like. Going live can also be a popular way of senior people making a big announcement.

You will need to do some planning to ensure these sessions are a success. Here are some suggested steps to help you prepare.

Promote ahead of time

A sudden, ad hoc live piece of content can be a great way to excite your audience. Most of the time, however, you will benefit from promoting it well in advance, especially if there's a Q&A element. Whether it's a one-off live or a regular series, make sure you promote it in advance with compelling videos and social media imagery. If your event is on a Friday, start plugging it at least the Monday before.

Brief the people involved

You've got to ensure everyone is on the same page. Explain why the live is happening, what success looks like, the other people involved and the technology needed. This doesn't need to be a big formal meeting, but it's always good to make sure everyone is aware of the plan. This doesn't apply just to the people 'on screen' for the live content but to all the people directly involved. Bluntly, if something goes wrong, it also helps you by showing that you prepared thoroughly and briefed everyone.

Do a test run

Going live can be very nerve-racking, especially for the people on screen. You want to bring the best out of people – if they appear anxious, the audience will pick up on it and it's ultimately just bad content. By doing a test run the main event will feel a lot more natural and it also allows you to discover any problems you weren't aware of previously. If the live event is taking place on video, you can get a feel for how the location looks and if you want to change anything.

You can also try to anticipate some of the questions you'll get from the people joining. If the subject being discussed is controversial, this is absolutely essential. You can use the traffic light system mentioned earlier to help guide your decisions on what sort of comments to engage with.

Triple check your kit

Perhaps the sub-heading should just be 'Check your battery'. This is from bitter personal experience as these things drain faster than you plan for. If your battery on your camera runs out, the live content will draw to a very quick close. There's no need to use loads of equipment, but you want to make sure it's all working and that it's close to hand. If you're streaming live from a phone or laptop, your battery will drain very quickly. You may want to consider bringing a battery and/or signal booster.

Do you have a disaster plan?

You always want to aim for success but plan for failure. If something does go wrong in a live environment and there isn't a plan in place, things will unravel very quickly (and publicly). Again, if the subject matter you're dealing with is controversial, you have to think about what happens if something goes wrong. This could be being bombarded with negative comments, a piece of kit failing, a crucial person not turning up in time or someone in the content misbehaving. You don't need to have a giant folder with detailed plans for every possible problem, but at the very least think about what the realistic risks are and what you would do should they happen.

A mini disaster plan could include pre-written responses to likely negative comments, allowing you to reply quickly on the move. For failing kit your plan should include what equipment you are bringing as backup and what possibly needs to be purchased. If someone important doesn't turn up, whom will you put in their place (if at all?). It's also worth establishing your 'red lines' that would cause you to pull the live completely.

How will you measure success?

You could run a popular live content event with your audience that gets loads of views. But if your live content is designed to sell your products and it leads to only a handful of sales, has it been truly successful? Think carefully about what metric you will use to measure the event's success. This allows you to review and modify your plans as you schedule more live content.

The rise of messaging apps

For many years, people mainly used social media to broadcast everything out to the world. Over time, however, people came to realize the risks of doing this. Potential employers could dig through drunken photo albums, parents could spy on their teenage offspring, and embarrassing youthful haircuts could be seen by all for years to come. As a reaction to this, private networks and messaging apps became more and more popular (think of the rise of Snapchat). People could still communicate with their friends but in a much more secure way. This poses an obvious challenge if you're trying to build a community. How can you do that when more and more people are communicating with each other through closed-off apps and networks?

Thankfully, messaging apps also provide opportunities for audience building and community engagement. For starters, people expect to communicate with brands, organizations and public figures through the same messaging platforms. Think of how a lot of people use Twitter DMs or Facebook messages to send complaints or questions to organizations. By actively using these messaging apps and speaking to your audience as much as possible through them, you can build a highly personable and engaged group of followers.

What's more, these same platforms allow people to be a lot more candid. If you work for a public health organization, people are very likely to share details of their medical problems or ask questions about them on a public social media platform. But you could use messaging apps to allow people to ask questions directly. They would be more willing to share candid stories or thoughts if they can do this anonymously. A famous example of this is Postsecret, where people mail incredibly candid secrets anonymously to be published online.

If you are interested in journalism, private messaging apps offer a fantastic opportunity to help you with news gathering. If you build an audience that trusts you and can contact you through private messaging apps, you can securely receive tip-offs and story ideas.

When I helped launch Forces TV, a UK channel, I set up a WhatsApp daily news alert that people could sign up to. Every day they would receive an update with all the latest stories. Initially it was just meant to broadcast out to people and help push up traffic to the website. Something really interesting started to happen, though – people would start asking for more information about particular stories, sharing their thoughts on the headlines and sharing their own experiences. It became an invaluable source of news and content, while our audience felt engaged and listened to.

Even if messaging apps don't strike you as a crucial part of your content strategy, they are virtually always helpful to it in some way.

User-generated content

The focus of this book is about you and your organization producing content. I hope you won't be offended by the notion that you can't produce all of it. Your audience is a never-ending potential source of great stories, photos and videos. The popularity of smartphones means that all of them can instantly capture and send you imagery of current events.

In stark commercial terms, this content is also free. You cannot be everywhere at once, and by harnessing the content produced by your audience you can gather high-quality imagery for little to no cost. Do be clear with people who send it to you, though – if your audience feels tricked, it will quickly abandon you.

Ask for and use this content to augment your own. This improves not only the quality of your material but also its authenticity. It could be pictures from a breaking news event, people's advice on a particular issue, or them speaking about what makes them passionate. You can take this to the next level by regularly planning UGC events and rewarding the best submissions. A classic example of this is *National Geographic* featuring photos from its readers. People compete to appear in such a prestigious magazine while the publishers benefit from stunning photography.

The best content is ultimately conversational rather than just broadcasting out and hoping people listen. You are likely to find that people will send you their content whether you ask for it or not. Do get people's consent, though. Even if they send it to you, make sure you go back and ask them if it's OK to publish widely. You should also verify UGC (especially in a news environment). People may be misinformed or sending you fraudulent material. While they may own the content, it may be footage of someone else who has not given consent to being filmed or their image being shared. By speaking to the person who sent it you can find out the details of how it was produced.

User-generated content will often surprise you. People are incredibly creative in ways that are impossible to plan for. By getting more people to submit content to you, you're using that rich network of creative ideas.

Influencers

Once you've started to build up an audience and gather some user-generated content, you may notice that a few people who follow you are particularly influential. They could be someone your analytics show frequently shares your content to a large number of followers. They could be a very vocal member of your forum who is popular with other members. It could even be that annoying person who criticizes your content – but in an accurate way.

Working with these influencers is taking user-generated content to the next level. By identifying these people you can amplify all your content and messaging through them. Let's say you work for a company that's launched a new fitness product. The brand already has a big social media following with a handful of particularly enthusiastic customers. When the product is launched you're required to produce promotional digital content.

But if you produce only your own content you would be missing a valuable opportunity. Why not get in touch with these enthusiasts and offer them an early trial of the product in exchange for them producing video reviews to share with their friends and your followers?

This has a number of advantages over your own content. It would be valued more by people interested in your brand, as an honest review is obviously more authentic and trustworthy than outright marketing material. The video reviews would take you little time or cost to arrange, and would make your already supportive followers even more positive.

There will always be angry people online leaving pointless negative comments. You may find content you publish is perceived very badly. Serious problems could be identified by your audience, or high-profile people may criticize your work with credible points made. The natural human reaction is to ignore or dismiss these negative responses. But to truly improve your content and create a loyal audience you have to fix what you're doing wrong. You could get in touch with some of these people and ask for more detailed thoughts. It might be hard, but it will improve what you're doing.

Influencers don't have to be people already following you. Let's go back to the new fitness product example. You should research who the most influential people online in the world of fitness are. It could be social media celebrities, fitness video bloggers or sports writers. You could contact them and see if they will use or review your new product. This gets your content in front of an entirely new audience of potential customers. The biggest digital influencers would expect payment to promote a product, but you don't have to work only with the people with the largest audiences. Someone with a small but loyal audience who is willing to review your product could be an enormous boost to your work.

Authenticity has become one of the most important measures of effective communications. People are becoming less swayed by glamorous, expensively produced adverts as they become more savvy about being advertised to. Peer review and authentic commentary are instead the most trusted form of content. So by working with influencers and giving them a voice you can help ensure your content is as authentic as possible.

When things go wrong

So far we have focused on the positives of community building (and rightly so, you should feel encouraged). Sadly, at some point, something will inevitably go wrong. No matter how much you plan, or how safe you make your content, you simply won't get it right every time. While it can feel incredibly stressful at the time, it's ultimately one of the most important ways you'll learn; take it from someone who has made pretty much every mistake you can think of.

The speed of digital communications can make these mistakes feel even more scary. You proudly publish the content you've spent ages working on, only to see angry comments pour in after the audience spot an embarrassing typo. You might be sending content to social media while rushing, and accidentally publish personal photos from your phone instead.

More seriously, you could publish something that looked innocent in production but that people find inappropriate or offensive when it appears. You may manage the social channels for a large company that is suddenly embroiled in a major controversy.

While working with influencers can be an effective communications technique, it is not without risk. Influencers would expect to have editorial control of their content and it may not be suitable for your audience. If the content they produce backfires, it could reflect badly on your brand. You should work only with influencers whom you trust and know well.

While small- or large-scale problems are inevitable, there are things you can do to help prevent them.

Editorial judgement

The importance of building up editorial judgement has come up a few times now. This sense will help prevent inappropriate content getting published. When you're posting, it's worth asking yourself a few simple questions. Could this content be misinterpreted? Is it appropriate for the target audience? Is it published at an appropriate time? You wouldn't want to publish comedic material during a remembrance event, for example. Your editorial judgement of what content is right for your audience will be your best defence.

Check the security of your channels

Accounts being hacked is becoming more and more of a problem on social media. It can range from the mildly embarrassing (an annoyed ex-employee posting a rant to the company page) to the complete PR disaster (the White House's social media channels being hacked by terrorists). Make sure your accounts are as secure as possible. All the social media companies have public advice on making your account secure – read it. It's also worth carefully managing who has access to your channels and reviewing regularly.

Second pair of eyes

No matter what attention to detail you have, mistakes will always slip through. It could be typos, jump cuts or factual inaccuracies. Always get someone else to have a quick look at the content you've produced. This also helps get a second opinion on the content itself and covers you in case there is a problem with the content once it's published.

Know your audience

What is right and appropriate in terms of content is different for each audience. The importance of knowing your audience returns here, as you need to develop a sense of what content will work and what would cause a backlash. You have to take creative risks and try pushing the boundaries while giving your audience what they want. Something that's easier said than done.

Learn from your mistakes

Own up to your mistakes, look back at exactly what happened and figure out what you can do to prevent it happening again. It could be improving your internal processes, speaking to your audience more, or not using a particular style of content.

Exercise

This exercise is designed to encourage you to start building your own online community. Even one that is small and niche can be enormously successful and will give you experience as well as providing tangible proof to employers that you have this much sought-after skill. It shows in practical terms that you can successfully build a digital audience.

First, identify a subject you're passionate about. It could be a hobby such as hockey or board games or issues in your local community.

Then create a community content strategy. Plan the following:

1 What mix of digital channels are you going to use?

2 What content can you produce to engage that audience?

3 What size audience do you want to build?

4 How will you measure your success?

After you have done this, get busy and create that community. You will have to do some 'real-world' marketing to help build it, but hopefully you have people with whom you share your passions who can help get you started.

Once you have done this and have gained a small number of followers, try to plan either a live, interactive content event or a themed campaign for which you produce specific content.

Your efforts will be successful and, combined with the other exercises, you'll not only have great content examples but also evidence of audience growth too, making you a lot more employable.

Summary

So now you should understand the value of working closely with your audience. It's all too easy to just broadcast out to the world and never have a conversation with the people who are listening to you. But by doing so you can ensure your efforts will be successful.

As we have looked at content creation itself and then at developing an audience, we shall now look at actually measuring the success (or not) of our content.

Evaluation 06

- The only way to know if you're successful is through effective evaluation.
- Analytics can tell you a huge amount about your content (and your audience).
- Beware of vanity metrics and reading the wrong signals.

Up until this point we have focused on the production of content. Perhaps you've made a powerful video, built a digital audience and published your video on your social media channels. You might think that it's now time to put your feet up – but sadly it's not time to relax yet.

Evaluation, based on credible data, is the only way you'll ever know if what you're doing is actually working. Think about the rise of digital advertising. In the past, if you put an advert in the local newspaper or ran an expensive TV ad, you would have no real way of measuring how effective it was. It would have been possible to measure increases in sales around the time of advertising campaigns, but certainly nothing much more sophisticated than this. You were also very limited in your ability to target your advertising to particular people. With digital advertising you can do both – accurately target specific audiences and measure how popular your advert is with them. It's not that surprising, therefore, that advertising spend on 'traditional' media is dramatically falling.

Detailed evaluation allows you to measure a very wide array of different things about your content. It could range from the number of views your content has had to detailed audience insights.

Proper evaluation is something you have to build into every content and campaign plan you create. Deciding which metrics to measure and what your targets are should be second nature. Evaluation is also important if you're running a team of content producers. Without detailed metrics, you'll be unable to provide guidance and insight on what's working. Evaluation also lets you spot audience trends that you can then use. You might discover people are interested in a subject you hadn't previously considered, thanks to your audience insights.

Choosing the right metrics is arguably the most important part of evaluation. A video may quickly gather a vast number of initial views. But the analytics tell you that because it has a very compelling opening shot, people are watching for a few seconds and then switching off. The initial video views may be high, but only 2 per cent per cent of viewers watched all the way to the end. Was the video therefore successful? If you had picked initial views as your metric, the video would have been an enormous success (according to your plan). Sadly, though, it clearly isn't effective – most people watched for only a few seconds.

In this situation, a better metric would have been to measure 10 or 30 second views. This number gives you a more accurate picture of how many people watched in a meaningful way. You can also use this information to improve your content in future. If you saved the crucial bit of information until the end of the video, the overwhelming majority of people who watched would have missed it. So from now on, you know to put the vital information at the start of the video.

Demonstrating to an employer that you can evaluate content effectively complements your content production skills. Too often people focus on the production of the content itself, but by demonstrating you can evaluate too you'll stand out from the crowd.

But what is proper evaluation? Because of the wealth of information available to you, it's all too easy to get swamped with numbers. Good evaluation should:

- measure the success (or failure) of your content against your objectives;
- provide insight you can use to improve your content in future;
- measure inputs as well as outputs;
- be transparent.

We'll now discuss each of these points in detail to explain why each one matters.

Why producing great stuff is only half the job

Demonstrating that your content is effective isn't just important for your own satisfaction. You may have to show your digital editor why the content you have produced is popular with audiences. You may produce content for a commercial client and need to deliver against set objectives. If you are running a public sector or charitable campaign, you have to evaluate your content to show it's an effective use of money.

Let's cover the fundamentals of what good evaluation should be.

Measure the success (or failure) of your content against your objectives

Before producing content as a one-off or as part of a long-term campaign, it's important to set objectives. These don't need to be complicated or numerous, but you need to define success. Sometimes these objectives will be obvious – if you want to produce advertising content that gets a certain number of people clicking through to a website, the number of clicks is the most important objective to measure. You need to be specific in your evaluation: it's tempting just to think 'if my content is popular then it's done the job'. Setting objectives for you and your team makes sure you are focusing on what your content is meant to achieve.

The SMART criteria can help you set effective objectives. They are shown in the table.

Table 6.1   SMART objectives for measuring content effectiveness

	SMART	Not
Specific	We want to reach 18- to 21-year-old men interested in fitness	We want to reach young people
Measurable	Get 20,000 video views	Inspire people
Achievable	We got 20,000 engagements before so we want 25,000 this time	Wouldn't it be great if we got a billion visits

(Continued)

Table 6.1 *(Continued)*

	SMART	Not
Relevant	We are launching a new website so we're measuring unique visitors	We are launching a new website so we're measuring retweets
Timely	The content has to get more views than our average in 24 hours	As long as it gets the views at some point were happy

By getting into the habit of using SMART objectives you'll ensure you're on the right track when it comes to producing content. Regularly reviewing these objectives is also recommended as your goals may change over time.

Provide insight

This book certainly doesn't have all the answers, and what's right for one audience can be very different for another. If you are working in a team, it's especially important that you regularly review your work and how it's resonating with your target audiences. 'You produced a really beautiful design' may be flattering, but how useful is it?

Effective evaluation should include valuable insight into what you can do better next time. Every review or evaluation document should include a 'lessons learnt' section. It doesn't have to be rocket science – a simple lesson is still a valuable one. For example, you may be running a long-term campaign involving lots of different media types. Once it's complete you review the analytics, which show that animations were generally watched all the way through, while the audience switched off videos after a few seconds.

So the simple lesson learnt would be to produce more animations next time, as they were more useful to the target audience. This also neatly illustrates that evaluation doesn't have to be done at the end of the campaign. If you have the time, it's best to do it on an ongoing basis. Why wait until you're done to improve your work?

Finally, it's worth sharing these insights as widely as you can. In the world of digital content, people are always sharing ideas about what does or doesn't work. It's also a great way to raise your profile within your industry if people start to see you as a reliable source of fresh insight.

Measure inputs as well as outputs

It's all well and good measuring whether the content you've made is effective or not. But how much time did it take to produce? What was the cost?

If you're running your own business, this should be second nature. You'll be used to measuring the cost to profit benefit to everything you do, and content shouldn't be any different. Evaluate how much of your resources your content has taken. It's not worth doing this for everything you make (unless it's highly complex), but it's certainly worth reviewing.

This is critical if you're managing a team. You have to monitor how much of their time content takes to produce and whether it's worth it. Why get two people to produce a complex piece of story-telling over a number of days if the audience prefers a quick video interview filmed and broadcast live? Effective content isn't just material that's popular with your audiences but also content that doesn't place a heavy burden on your limited resources.

Be transparent

This can be difficult. You may put your heart and soul into a powerful piece of content that then falls completely flat with your audience. It's never easy to admit failure or that you've made a mistake. But evaluation works both ways – it gives you a solid foundation to promote your successes but also highlights where you haven't achieved your goals. You shouldn't take this personally, and by identifying the lessons learnt you still learn and grow.

Hold regular meetings with your team to review the content you've produced that week or that month. If everyone is transparent about what worked and what didn't, you can ensure your long-term success as you'll be able to absorb new findings quickly.

Commonly used terms explained

There are a number of different terms that are used in digital evaluation. It's important to understand the nuance of each one so that you are confident in reviewing your work. Unhelpfully, different social networks or tools use slightly different measurements. Reach on Facebook is not the same as impressions on Twitter, although they may look similar.

In this section you will find an explanation of the most commonly used phrases as well as guidance on which metrics are good and bad for measuring.

Bounce rate

Bounce rate is a metric used for websites. It's the percentage of people who leave your website after looking at only one page. Generally you want this to be as low as possible. If you have a high bounce rate, it suggests that people find your site either boring or unhelpful.

There is not a set 'good' bounce rate – this is another metric you should measure over time and try to lower. Generally it would be extremely hard to get it below 25 per cent, while over 60 per cent would be bad. If you find that your site does suffer from a high bounce rate, you can try improving the content, improving the design to make it easier to navigate or check you are targeting the right audiences. Speed is also a big deal – if your website loads slowly and has lots of intrusive popups, people will simply leave.

Use it for seeing if your website is working properly for your audience.

Avoid ignoring this metric.

Clickthroughs

Clickthroughs are the number of people who visited your website from your content. It could simply come from an e-mailed or tweeted link, an embedded 'visit us' button in your video or from an advertising campaign. These are expressed as either the number of clickthroughs or the clickthrough rate (CTR), which is the number of clicks as a percentage of the people who saw the content.

This is a very important metric, especially if you're running a paid-for advertising campaign. If you're paying to try to boost traffic to your website, this is the number you should be keeping an eye on. A low CTR would suggest the content isn't clear or compelling. A high CTR naturally says the opposite.

Use it for measuring how effective your content is at sending traffic to your website.

Avoid only measuring it when you are running an advertising campaign. It's worth checking how good your content is at sending traffic to your site even when you aren't promoting it.

Engagements

Engagements is a very important metric – it shows you how many people responded to your post or content. This includes adding a comment, liking it, sharing it, following you as a result of seeing it, or negative things such as reporting or unfollowing you. It shows how interesting your content is, as people have taken the time to respond in some way.

Having a very large number of engagements may not necessarily be a good thing. If you post content that your followers absolutely loathe, yes, you'll have an incredible engagement rate, but it doesn't mean you have a happy audience. Generally though, you want your audience as engaged as possible, but make sure you review what those engagements are to ensure you're on the right track.

Use it for analysing how interested your audience is in your content. Look into the stats in detail to see how people respond differently to your content.

Avoid assuming all engagements are positive.

Engagement rate

The engagement rate is the number of engagements as a percentage of impressions. So if you had 1,000 impressions and 100 engagements, your engagement rate would be 10 per cent. There is no global average – you have to figure out what yours is over time and then try to improve on it. Generally though, 1–2 per cent is a good rule of thumb.

Use it for setting a benchmark to measure how your content performs and see how your audience becomes more or less active over time.

Avoid assuming that all the engagements that make up your engagement rate are positive.

Impressions

The number of time a post or piece of content has been seen. This isn't the number of people who have seen a post, as someone could see the same content a number of times. This is often the largest number your metrics will show you.

Use it for a way to measure the overall distribution of your content and awareness of your brand.

Avoid using it to demonstrate how effective your content is. Many people may have seen it, but if none of them actually view it, it isn't effective at all.

Organic and paid

Social media is funded through advertising. If you're running a page on social media, you will have the option either to post normally or to pay to boost the post to more people. In your analytics you will see this separated out as organic, ie those that were not boosted, and as advertising and paid posts that were. A general rule of thumb is that it's sensible to boost content that's already performing well organically with your audience, as you know it's popular.

Pageviews

Pageviews are similar to impressions. It simply means how many times your website has been looked at. Note that it is different from uniques. Pageviews is the number of views, not the number of people looking at the page. So if you have a popular news site that people check daily, your pageviews will be much higher than your uniques.

Use it for measuring how popular your site or parts of it are. You can also use it to demonstrate the site's worth to advertisers and how compelling your content is.

Avoid using it to measure how effective specific pieces of content are.

Reach

Reach is simply the number of people who have seen a piece of content. This is different from impressions – one person may view a post ten times but that still counts as one reach measure. It's generally slightly lower than impressions owing to repeat views from your followers. You should measure how much your reach is increasing (or decreasing) over time to see how widely your content is being seen.

Use it for a way to measure the overall distribution of your content and awareness of your brand.

Avoid using it to demonstrate how effective your content is (as for impressions).

Sentiment

Sentiment is the measurement of what people think of your content, brand or subject. Obviously, it would take an incredibly long time to manually go through every comment and figure out what percentage is positive or negative. Thankfully, there are a number of powerful analytical tools that can do this automatically by studying the language people use. This, combined with your engagement metrics, gives you a much more detailed picture of how your content is performing.

Word clouds are often created by these tools. They show you what phrases people use along with your content. This can help you identify trends and what your audience is interested in. Sadly, sentiment analysis isn't that simple – despite the power of analytical tools, they are not perfect. For instance, they cannot detect sarcasm and often tag such comments as positive. Therefore any sentiment analysis should be combined with some human analysis. It can be as simple as someone checking any automated sentiment analysis and making sure it's got things right. Categorize comments or content into supportive, negative and indifferent to get an idea of what your audience's mood is like.

Use it for learning more about what your audience thinks and what subjects they are passionate about.

Avoid taking raw sentiment analysis data at face value.

Uniques

Uniques are sometimes also called users. This number can be a confusing one, but it's as close as you can measure to the number of people visiting your website. What makes life tricky is that most people have multiple devices and browsers. For example, you may have a work computer, a personal tablet and a smartphone. By the end of the day you may have visited your favourite news site on all these devices. The analytics would measure this as three uniques or users – despite you being one person!

Use it for measuring how many people visit your website (in an imperfect way), tracking the growth of your audience, and comparing it to the pageviews to see how many people are returning to your site.

Avoid thinking it equates to the exact number of people visiting your site. It's essential you measure it alongside pageviews too, so you can see how loyal your audience is.

Video views

You may think this does what it says on the tin – how many people have seen your video. Sadly, it's not that simple. What actually counts as a video view? Different platforms measure views in different ways. When Facebook announced their new video player, they measured three seconds as a view. Most videos on Facebook autoplay, so it's likely that each one would get three seconds of view time as people scroll past, so it's not a helpful number. YouTube measures around 30 seconds as a view. Therefore it's important to check carefully how the platform you're using measures views.

If your platform provides it, keep a close eye on retention – how long people are watching. This is usually depicted as a graph. If people drop off suddenly at a particular place in the video, try to establish why.

Use it for measuring how many people watched your video.

Avoid just measuring the initial view number. Look at how many people watched for 10 or 30 seconds.

CASE STUDY Alex Aiken, Executive Director of
Government Communications

The Government Communications Service is the professional body of communicators for the UK government. They have made evaluation a top priority over the past few years. I spoke to Alex Aiken about how communications have changed in recent years and what skills he looks for in professional government communicators.

The Government Communication Service (GCS) is the professional body for people who work in communications within the UK government. Government communications in the UK have now existed for over 100 years. Originally GCS was known as the Department for Information, which was founded in 1917 and hired John Buchan as its first director. This was the start of a long history of government using creative messaging to tell an important story.

The biggest changes that we've seen in communication are related to people's habits. As a result of the developments in online communications, we now have direct channels through which to provide people with information but, crucially, these people now have direct channels such as social media through which they can interact with us too. There is so much more conversation now. This ability to communicate straight to the public has been highly valuable, particularly in immediate scenarios like crisis communications. However, GCS have also done brilliant long-term campaigns with the aid of direct communications, such as the anti-drink-driving campaign THINK (which aims to save lives) and the GREAT Britain campaign (which promotes the UK as a place to visit and do business).

What people joining GCS require is a passion for public service. Just being able to use Facebook well will not get them very far. If they can develop an understanding of how communications can be used in public service to inspire and empower people, they will thrive. I always tell people that what we're looking for is a passion for public service. It's not just about creating the most brilliant bit of digital content – it's about serving the public good.

Following on from that, it is also really important to have a positive attitude and a desire to learn. Communications channels are multiplying and the industry is in constant change. A communications professional needs to understand emerging forms of communication and be able to build successful coalitions quickly. This requires a curiosity to learn as well as the ability to apply new knowledge through hard work and attention to detail.

Evaluation is what allows us to be transparent and show value to the taxpayer. For example, £10 million was spent on the 2016 Stoptober campaign: a campaign designed to help people stop smoking. Evaluation allows people to have confidence that departments are doing everything they can to ensure their communications are effective and the money is well spent. For this particular campaign, if more people give up smoking, fewer people will die of smoking-related diseases. Data showed that the campaign had a direct effect on the number of people giving up smoking when asked why they did so.

I don't believe in instinctive communications: I believe in scientific communications – the analysis of data, use of case studies, and measurement. To understand how it works, you need evaluation tools. It requires first-class human intelligence to assess and analyse the data and understand the motivations of people. In public service communication, this matters because we have to demonstrate value from our work.

Common mistakes

When it comes to evaluation, the biggest mistake most people make is simply not doing any. So by doing even the simplest analysis of your content you're already doing well. As this section covers, it's important to get into the habit of regularly reviewing your and your team's content to make sure you know it's working properly.

But it's easy to spend a lot of time evaluating, so you want to make sure you avoid some of these mistakes.

Vanity metrics

When you first see the stats for your digital content, it's completely natural to look for the biggest numbers. If you've published a video on social media, your reach will be higher than the number of video views – and certainly the 10- or 30-second views. The latter is more meaningful, but it feels nice to promote the big number to people you work with.

It's important to resist this temptation. You ideally want all your stakeholders to understand the importance of choosing the right metrics. If you've trained them properly, they will see through your ploy to pick the big number.

You should be especially vigilant about vanity metrics when there's money involved. Unscrupulous digital agencies may try to show you just the biggest numbers to make themselves look good. This can be avoided by setting SMART objectives and being clear with other organizations about what metrics matter.

Vanity metrics can have a place, though – if you're trying to convince a busy, senior manager of the value of digital content, sometimes you have to dazzle with big numbers rather than explain the nuances of digital measurement. But use them very sparingly.

Using sledgehammers to crack nuts

With the market for digital analytics growing rapidly, there is a wide range of extremely powerful analytical packages out there. These hoover up vast amounts of data, can perform highly complex analysis and visualize data in an appealing way.

Despite what their salespeople will tell you, these packages require a lot of training and skill to use effectively. They are also very expensive. Many organizations or teams see them as a shortcut to brilliant evaluation, but without plenty of training this can be a waste of time. They are often too powerful for what most teams need to actually measure, and with their complexity it's hard for everyone to understand the reports. Clearly, though, they have a place, especially if you can assign dedicated evaluators to manage them, but the free analytics provided by the social networks or websites will do the job for the vast majority of people, so think carefully before investing in an all-singing, all-dancing evaluation package.

Not enough data

When you want to do any meaningful user research, it's important you gather enough data to make it as accurate as possible. For example, if you want to survey your audience to find out what content they want more or less of, you won't get much meaningful data by asking ten people. As a bare minimum you should always try to survey at least 1,000 people. This can obviously make it harder and more expensive, but you can trust the data that way. If you want to increase the number of people taking part in your research, you may want to offer an incentive or outsource to a specialist company.

Meaningful user research should be the foundation of any digital project. If you are building a new website, launching a new media brand or developing an app, you can't just assume what the users will want and how they will use it.

Too much data

It's easy to get swamped by spreadsheets. This is a similar mistake to using overly complex analytical tools. By just harvesting large quantities of data you're not helping anyone. If you're going to capture data, have you planned how you will analyse them? Also consider whether you need to bring in any specialists to help evaluate the material.

Specializing as an evaluator

Digital content provides a rare mix of the artistic and the scientific – you can produce beautiful content that tells a powerful story while also subjecting it to rigorous evaluation. You may want to consider specializing as an evaluator if it's something you enjoy and have a talent for. People with solid evaluation skills are in big demand and you can learn a lot of the skills yourself.

It's worth being comfortable with evaluation skills no matter what aspect of digital content you're interested in, but don't discount it as a great career choice in itself. So what overall skills would you need?

Organized and strategic How are you going to solve people's evaluation problems? You'll need to produce and carry out a successful plan.

Listening and observing What people do and what people say are often two different things. Knowing how to analyse the difference is important.

Analytical and objective You'll inevitably be working with a lot of data. You'll have to be able to study them and find valuable insights from them too.

Communication and collaboration You could answer that these are crucial skills for any role. And you'd be right. But it's not good enough just to understand the data – you have to work with people with different skills from many different teams. Can you explain the data clearly? Can you repurpose them for different needs?

Empathy This goes a long way in understanding people.

So what evaluation roles are there? Here are some examples.

Digital marketing analyst

Advertising companies, digital agencies and in-house marketing teams usually have a large digital analysis team. You'll be measuring the effectiveness of campaigns and paid-for advertising, and conducting audience research. You should spend the time to become a Google Analytics pro as well as studying one other large analytics package. Your employers would want you to demonstrate whether adverts are performing well, how customers (or potential customers) are discovering and interacting with marketing material, and how marketing content can be altered to appeal to more people.

You'll need a range of skills, including SEO and HTML knowledge, on top of your content skills. You'll also spend a lot of time performing audits for clients or colleagues. Not only do you need to be able to perform these audits, but you also need to be able to convey your findings clearly.

User researcher

User research is a complex skill and one that's highly in demand. You'll need to learn how to conduct user testing, large-scale surveying or interviews, how to work with designers to ensure user interfaces work properly, and overall usability testing.

The best user research isn't just an initial fact-finding exercise. It should be an ongoing process to fine-tune digital products and services.

A huge range of organizations want to hire user researchers, which would give you a lot of choice in your career. You would generally be in demand from digital development companies, government agencies that provide digital services and large companies with a big digital presence.

Data scientist

Becoming a data scientist is academically challenging and would certainly require a qualification in a field such as computer science. These professionals can capture, sort and analyse vast quantities of highly complex information. It's not just academic ability you'll need, but also business nous. Knowing how your work fits into the overall goals of the organization will help you succeed. You'll need coding ability as well as database expertise. It's a challenging field, but a highly rewarding one: if you get a role as a data scientist, you could be working on AI research at a leading tech company.

Using evaluation to encourage

The transparency of digital analytics can make plenty of people nervous. Knowing that all the digital content you produce can be analysed in a wide variety of ways can make it feel as if any mistakes you make will be out in the open for everyone to see.

It's important to acknowledge this worry that people working for you may have. Of course, it's only right that thorough evaluation should underpin the content you produce. But this doesn't mean trying to catch people out. A sense of creativity and risk taking is crucial to any digital content team, a result of which means that inevitably some content will miss the mark.

Evaluation is actually an excellent way to encourage your team and foster some friendly competition. This book has recommended regular content meetings a number of times, and sharing the data on how content has performed should be a central part of them.

Here are some suggestions on how you can do this.

Weekly team update

Schedule a regular update with your team which uses your analytics to inform the discussion. People should share what worked and what didn't, identify what lessons were learnt and explore whether any surprises were found. If you have access to evaluation tools, it's worth putting them on a screen for all to see while the discussion takes place. It's often good to feature a set number of productions each week, so people have something to aspire to. You shouldn't just highlight the most popular content but also reward creativity, taking a risk, or thinking quickly in a fast-moving situation.

Monthly department update

Digital evaluation should be shared as widely as possible. It's worth hosting brief highlight sessions with your wider department or organization if possible. Not only does this let you and your team plug the great work you've been doing, but it also allows as many people as possible to learn from your work. Everyone benefits from having a greater understanding of your audiences and the methods that successfully appeal to them.

You probably don't want to air your metaphorical dirty laundry at these updates – you can save that for the team-only meetings – but you should be as open as possible. The lessons you have learnt and the insights you have gained are particularly valuable discussion points for these sessions.

Visualization screens

If possible, it's a worthy investment to put some screens around the office showing analytics, content that's currently being distributed, and what your audience are discussing. In newsrooms it's absolutely worth sharing what the most popular/discussed articles currently are. Likewise in PR offices or communications offices, keeping a word cloud or other form of live data displayed has the benefits of giving people immediate insight and reminding them that these tools are available to use if they need them.

You don't necessarily need fancy analytical tools. You can simply design your own graphics and update them on, say, a weekly basis.

Regular e-mail bulletin

In a large, complex organization you obviously can't share all your successes and insights face to face. You may consider sharing a regular e-mail bulletin about your most successful content with relevant stakeholders. Or if you're feeling really digital, update your internal social media or chat apps.

You might consider producing a regular bulletin that anyone can sign up to. This is a great way to improve your and your organization's reputation for digital leadership – although obviously be careful about what information you share.

Rewards

As always, rewards are a brilliant way to motivate people. You could have a trophy that changes hands every week, vouchers for coffees, or even go back to school with some gold stars.

Exercise

So far, the exercises in this book have concentrated on actually producing the content. If you've been diligently following them (which I'm certain you have been), you should now have a collection of content that you have also published.

Helpfully, this provides the perfect foundation for this exercise. We are going to think about what objectives you could have set and how your content performed. If you haven't yet published any of your content, now is a good time to do so. If you're nervous about posting it publicly, you can still follow some of this exercise – you just won't have any real-world data to look at.

Stage one

Refer to the SMART objectives in Table 6.1. Which objectives can you set yourself using it? Think carefully about what you want to achieve – traffic to a website, awareness and so on – and then choose your objective appropriately. Make sure you consider each part of the table and fill in each section in Table 6.2.

Table 6.2   Blank SMART evaluation table

Specific
Measurable
Achievable
Relevant
Timely

Stage two

You should now have decided which metrics you want to measure according to your SMART objectives. So for website traffic you should be measuring the CTR, or for audience participation you should measure engagement and possibly sentiment. Once the content has been published, look at your analytics and evaluate how successful you have been:

1 Which goals did you exceed?

2 Which ones did you fall short of?

3 Most importantly, what are the lessons learnt from this?

Once you are publishing content for real, you should be going through this process as standard, so it's a great way to build up practical communications skills.

Summary

This chapter has demonstrated why it's important to evaluate, how to evaluate consistently to maintain standards, and how to specialize in the field. Good evaluation doesn't have to be complicated or require hefty qualifications.

Now that we have covered the production and measurement of digital content, we will move on to arguably the most important method of distributing it – social media.

Social media 07

- Social media is one of the most important communication methods in today's world.
- It's fast changing.
- Flexibility and creativity are the keys to success on social media.

As I explained in the introduction to this book, digital platforms are now the main way that most people communicate with each other. It's also how they talk to organizations and public figures. Writing letters, phoning helplines and watching TV adverts have been largely replaced with social media feeds and apps.

When friends have a complaint about a faulty product or poor customer service, I often tell them to tweet the organization responsible rather than phoning them or e-mailing. They get a quicker and more helpful answer because the organization knows their responses are public. It's in their interest to help the customer quickly and transparently. No one knows how long you've been kept on hold (unless you moan about it a lot). Recently, a colleague was horrified to find a large piece of sharp metal in a box of cereal. She couldn't get through to the company's helpline. After tweeting a photo of the metal plate, she got a response within 30 seconds.

People also use their social media newsfeeds as important sources of news and information rather than just updates from their friends and family. The Reuters Institute Digital News report published in 2016 shows that people up to the age of about 45 get most of their news from digital sources.

So digital platforms have two important functions: to be sources of information and to help people communicate. Understanding how people share and respond to information is essential to succeeding at digital content.

In this chapter, as in the rest of the book, I will not be explaining how to use specific social networks. It might seem odd, but there wouldn't be any point: social networks emerge and change so quickly. By the time you're reading this, any specific advice could simply be out of date. What I will focus on here are the fundamental lessons that you need to learn in order to succeed at social media. These lessons apply no matter what network you're using.

But what actually is social media? It's surprisingly hard to define. If we start out with social networks like Facebook, or older ones like Myspace, it can be simple. As an individual or organization you have a profile, you connect with other people, and you post content such as photos or videos (user-generated content). But what about more private social networks like Snapchat? Your profile can be anything you like. And what about messaging apps? These were not considered social media networks at first, until people realized they are still used to share stories, content and updates quickly through networks of people. Still, while the meaning of social media can be a little elusive, you shouldn't worry too much. If it feels like a social media network, then it is one.

The popularity of social media started before smartphones became commonplace, but it was hugely accelerated when everyone started having a device that could easily capture and share content. Many social networks are designed specifically around mobile – Instagram and Snapchat are famous examples. Just as the emergence of radio and the telegram changed how people communicated, so too did the rise of the smartphone.

The media traditionally had a lot of control over how people got their news and entertainment. They would schedule programmes at set times, have a set number of channels or stations, and dictate who could advertise on the platforms. Social media has completely changed this, as people now have access to an unlimited amount of content. It means that no matter how niche your interests, you will be able to connect with like-minded people and consume only the content you're interested in, wherever you want, at a time that suits you. To get a bit technical, the costs of the means of production and distribution of content have fallen to near zero. In the past, if you wanted to broadcast to the world, you'd need expensive equipment such as a TV studio or a radio station using complex technology that required a lot of training. Now, anyone can broadcast to the world from their smartphone.

This means that there are two important factors to consider when thinking about starting a career in digital content:

More freedom It used to be the case that if you wanted to do something creative or work in the media, you'd have to hound an established company for a job. Now, there is nothing stopping you producing your own content and sharing it with the world. Think of the popularity of video bloggers – they are modern-day celebrities without a record label or publicist. So if you want to create content, you can use social media to share it with the world – entirely free of charge. However...

It's more competitive This has the obvious result that more people than ever are producing content to an audience that is extremely discerning about what they want to see. Please do not be discouraged by this fact – if anything, it's good news for the creative producer. When there's a lot of noise, it pays to specialize in a niche audience or subject. Don't worry about chasing big numbers – think about building a highly engaged, passionate audience for a subject you feel strongly about. Perhaps you're interested in food, for example. Instead of creating a social media brand about food, why not focus on something more specific, such as healthy eating, cheap recipes, or cheese (a personal favourite). It will help you stand out from the crowd in busy social networks.

There is a huge demand for talented social media professionals. It can be a competitive field too. To stand out from the crowd, you'll need to show you can produce your own content (by following the exercises in this book you should end up with a portfolio you can use). You'll also need to show that you can manage and grow a digital audience. By creating your own social media brand and modestly growing it, you'll have practical evidence of this.

Mythbusting

There are some myths about social media that just won't go away, possibly because it's still a new(ish) way of communicating and people are still trying to figure it out. These myths aren't harmless though, and can send teams in completely the wrong direction. Keep an eye out for them and challenge them wherever possible.

Social media is just for young people

While it's true that young people communicate mainly through social media, it doesn't mean it's all about them. Once I introduced my sixty-something mother to Pinterest she couldn't get enough of it. A lot of organizations treat social media as their way to communicate with young people while forgetting other audiences, assuming that older people stick with newspapers or radio. People get most of their information from online sources up to the age of 45, with those older than that still consuming a lot of digital news. To state the obvious, this will change over time too, as more people grow up with social media as a fact of life. In practice, this means catering for different age groups through social media if you have a broad audience to reach, and not siloing social media as exclusively for your youth audiences.

This myth also has another pernicious effect – it can make people who aren't very young feel alienated or nervous about working with social media. By treating social media as exclusively for young people, those not in those age demographics may feel past it, or that they can't learn how to use social media effectively – total nonsense.

Social media is silly

'Social media is just photos of people's lunch and cats' is something often said. In a similar way to thinking that social media is just for young people, it's often also treated as light-hearted or facile. This is a big mistake and completely overlooks the obvious ways in which social media is used that change the course of history – consider the

Arab Spring, the US presidential elections and the fact that reporters often cover major stories on Twitter. It's simply a way of communicating. News websites range from deeply analytical financial news to made-up stories about aliens living on the moon. Television ranges from powerful documentaries and storytelling to shows based on people being dowsed in custard. Social media is the same – it's merely a platform for people to make of it what they will.

This myth often manifests itself in content strategies – we'll work with newspaper journalists for the big interview with our CEO but then publish a video of him playing a guitar solo on social media. Of course, humour and simplicity have an important place in digital content, but don't equate it with social media by default.

Social media is complicated

I don't want to do myself out of a job here, but the truth is it's easy to learn how social media works. People can get very nervous about it and believe they'll never get their heads around it. But learning how to use social networks isn't tricky – they are designed to be as user friendly as possible. Don't feel afraid of them. The hard bit is learning how to make great content, manage a team or brand, and handle a communications crisis. This situation isn't helped when social media 'experts' try to make it as inaccessible as possible, with complicated language and convoluted strategies designed to keep them in work. Social media is simply a new way of communicating that you can practise working with until you get it right. What's more, with analytics you can learn exactly what is and isn't working. When it comes to social media, don't let anyone frighten you.

People on social media have the attention span of a goldfish

This one does have an element of truth in it – but it's important to get it right. It's often said that social media has conditioned us all to have attention spans measuring in the milliseconds. But if this is true, why do people spend hours binge-watching streaming services? Why have long-form written storytelling and journalism enjoyed a resurgence? The truth is more subtle. When you have access to basically unlimited content you can be extremely selective. If something doesn't immediately grab your interest you can instantly find something else. Social media is used many times throughout the day for short spaces of time – while people are waiting for a train, during a quiet spot at work or while standing in a queue. They therefore want short bits of content to fill that time. So the reason people spend so long watching streaming services is that it's often extremely high-quality content and they are choosing to spend their time doing so. This means your content for social media should be concise and engaging. If it's a dry subject, get the useful message across as quickly and clearly as possible. If it's not engaging or useful, then why publish it at all?

Everyone has to be on social media

A controversial one, this, but it's worth asking. Being successful on social media takes time and effort. It can also bring huge benefits for little cost. Despite this, it won't work for every organization. Perhaps your audience simply doesn't use social media much, or you don't have the time to run it properly. Don't give in to pressure to create lots of social media channels; a focused social media strategy on a small number of channels will be much more effective.

Every organization I've worked with experiences the same problem – suddenly every department or team wants their own social media channels. They feel they have a unique message that isn't being represented on the main brand channels, or their product deserves its own identity. This can be extremely hard to manage, as you can suddenly end up with an enormous number of social media channels with totally different messages, mistakes being made, and the potential audience split across lots of different accounts. Finding the balance between one or two main channels or lots of different accounts is tricky to get right, and if you're the person in charge, you'll come under a lot of pressure to give people their own pages. Resist!

How to choose the right network

When starting out on social media, it can be daunting. Where do you begin? It can feel as if there are loads of social networks out there and you probably don't have the time to publish to all of them. Even if you did, it would probably be a mistake to try to be everywhere all the time.

Instead, it's important to develop a social media strategy before starting out. This will help you not only to choose which social networks you want to broadcast on but also how you will tailor your content for each one. Here's what you should consider.

What do you want to achieve?

Social media can often be treated just as a way to broadcast to people, without much thought given to why you are actually on it in the first place. By thinking about what you want to achieve, you instantly get much more direction about which networks are right for you. You can have more than one goal. For example, you may want to start a new business selling smoothies. You have three objectives you want from social media – initially to raise awareness of your product, to find out what customers want and to run advertising campaigns. These three objectives already mean that messaging apps probably won't work, as they won't allow you to advertise. You'll need a network that allows people to comment and interact with your brand page to get feedback. To raise awareness you'll need a network that allows people to share your content so it can reach new potential customers.

What audiences do you want to reach?

You can't go wrong by starting out with the audiences you want to reach and then working backwards. Most social networks are more popular among certain age groups or other demographics such as gender. There is plenty of research and information out there about the makeup of each network's overall audience. By matching your message and market to their best associated social network you'll be on the right track. Again, this helps you focus and only spend time working on networks that suit your needs.

How much time and what resources do you have?

This is an easy question to overlook, but there's no point in listing all the benefits of having a solid social media presence if you are frantically running your own business. Be realistic about how much time and effort you can dedicate to your social media strategy. It's better to focus on one or two really well. There are apps and services out there to make posting to social media easier, but use them as a helper rather than an enabler. It's also worth thinking about what training you may need to invest in for you and your team too.

What content can you produce for each one?

Once you've settled on which networks you are going to publish on, you'll need to think about what content you can produce for each one. They usually have different requirements – one video may need to be produced in different lengths, shapes or formats.

How will you measure success?

Being clear about what metrics you'll be paying close attention to means the whole team knows what matters. It helps keep you focused and ultimately to learn if your strategy is working. It's all about trial and error, so don't be discouraged if you find it hasn't worked how you'd hoped. Just try a different approach.

Don't be afraid to close social media accounts either. If it isn't working and you've tried many different approaches, it may just be the wrong channel or network for your organization. There's no shame in closing down accounts – if you can back it up with accurate and thoughtful analysis.

CASE STUDY   Polly Curtis, Editor-in-Chief at HuffPost UK

Polly was previously Director of Media at the British Red Cross and Digital Editor at The Guardian. *She's an experienced journalist who has worked throughout the entire rise of digital media. I spoke to her about news in a digital world and the skills she looks out for.*

When I first decided to become a reporter the crucial skill was a nose for a story. You also needed to know how to research, write and interview people – these were the bread and butter of being a journalist. This is still true but digital and social media have brought game-changing opportunities.

I began my career on the *Guardian* website, as a reporter in one of the earliest iterations of *The Guardian*'s digital operation. There were new jobs available reporting online but, at that time, they were entry-level jobs – a training ground really. My early aim was to move to the newsroom as a print journalist because this was where the best journalism was happening. It's hard to imagine that now. I think digital is where the most exciting journalism is happening now.

During my time at *The Guardian*, we were riding the wave of moving from being a UK-based newspaper to becoming a digital organization with multiple offices around the world. I was very much a traditional reporter, working as a political journalist and education editor. Nevertheless, it struck me that one of the most interesting and difficult questions of the time was about how we could successfully move on to the internet. How could we make sure that we had storytelling that was as powerful online as it was in print?

I moved from reporter to news editor to digital editor just as *The Guardian* itself was reinventing itself as a digitally-focused newsroom. There was some resistance to digital at the beginning, but *Guardian* journalists quickly saw the potential of digital. We were motivated by the impact of live news, how we could read the metrics about how our stories were being consumed in real time and engage with the audience through Twitter and Facebook. The analytics gave us a new perspective on our journalism and social engagement gave us the opportunity to have conversations with people reading our stories. Digital and social media all became an inextricable part of journalism.

At the Red Cross, I recruited people to our social media team who started out with a journalism background. The relationship between social media and journalistic abilities is a close one. We didn't want to simply say 'We're the

Red Cross and we're doing X, Y and Z'. We wanted to give people insight and fascinating stories.

Now, at HuffPostUK, I am leading a truly digitally-native newsroom. That excites me, because we are looking for the best and freshest ways of telling the stories we care about and always consider our audience at the heart of that. That's what digital really means to me – it's the fact that you have such a close relationship with your audience. You can see what stories move them and how they respond. It's a profound development from the print model.

Our priorities right now are about listening to the audience, giving them more of the original stories that we can see they crave and being relevant in their lives. That's about being real and authentic and trying to claw back trust that has been eroded across the media.

The role of the journalist has never been more important. It is the best journalists, like those at HuffPost, *The Guardian*, the BBC and *The New York Times*, who counter fake news. It's so important for there to be sources that people can trust – which also means there is even more pressure not to get things wrong.

Having that nose for a story is still the most important quality you need as a new journalist. Digital skills give you the ability to tell those stories, but it's still your instincts that will identify them. It's important to engage with your audience and be part of the conversation on social media. Doing this makes you a better storyteller. But also get out of the office, see the world, and report.

Going viral

Whenever I work with organizations to improve their digital efforts, I often hear the same two requests – we want to reach young people and we want to go viral.

But what does going viral actually mean, and is it a good thing for your organization? And do I have a secret formula to help you do it?

No is the answer – and don't believe anyone who tells you they do. Going viral usually means content on social media being rapidly shared by large numbers of people. This can be in a positive way – an inspirational video, a funny photo or story, or someone's big success. It can also be negative – an embarrassing or shocking update, a company posting something by mistake, or a major piece of bad news. Because people can instantly share content with their friends, it allows a post to be rapidly shared by increasing numbers of people.

The Dollar Shave Club is a good example of harnessing the power of viral social media in Chapter 5. Their video went viral, huge numbers of people saw it and sales skyrocketed.

Humour or shock value is often the basis of viral content. People love to laugh and be surprised, so it's often funny or shocking short videos that tend to do well. A lot of people understand this, so there's always a huge amount of content trying to break out into a larger audience.

By going down this route an organization can run into real trouble. First, is it appropriate for your organization to be producing this sort of content? It's likely it's completely different from your tone of voice and values. Second, if you do manage to go viral, you'll have some big numbers you can use to impress people. But are they of any real value? You will not be able to control the randomness of who sees the content and, even if they enjoy it, forgets it.

The biggest problem about focusing on going viral is that it's simply very, very difficult. It's something plenty of people want to do and therefore there's a lot of competition out there. Of course, it was worth the Dollar Shave Club doing it – their audience was essentially all adult men. But if you want to focus on a specific audience you're better off focusing on what content they enjoy rather than hoping something will get shared widely.

It's not entirely negative. Anything you do that is popular with a large number of people is of course a success. Just don't expect going viral to help you achieve your organization's goals.

Ultimately it all comes down to one of the most important parts of social media content – the *emotional hook*. While chasing after viral successes is nearly always a bad idea for organizations, understanding the importance of the emotional hook is crucial to succeeding on social media.

Emotional hooks

Why do people share things on social media? Why do they like or comment on one piece of content but not another?

The answer is the emotional hook. Content that provokes an emotional reaction is what makes people interact with it. There's a large range of emotions some content may trigger. It may make people laugh, happy, proud, angry or sad. They may want to share an inspiring story, a funny video, or a piece of news that they are angry about. Content that doesn't provide this hook often dwindles.

This need to provide emotional hooks brings a challenge for many organizations such as newsrooms or government. Your content may be incredibly important and credible. By shamelessly trying to manipulate people's emotions you would be betraying your values. It's also sometimes very hard to make important information (such as how to fill in your tax return properly) emotionally engaging.

It might be tempting to try to just go after highly emotional storytelling, but your audience will quickly tire of this. If your subject matter is dry but important, your best chance of success is by being as concise and as helpful as possible. Helpful content often performs well alongside more emotionally charged material. For journalists the commitment to truthful reporting is of course paramount. You're more likely to thrive by telling powerful stories than by chasing cheap emotional responses.

If the content you're planning doesn't have emotional resonance with your audience and isn't useful to them, you'll have to ask yourself a very hard question – is it worth publishing at all?

When people share something, they are doing it to say something about themselves. Sometimes it can be as benign as 'I care about this subject', or a bit more shameless such as showing off the posh restaurant they are lucky enough to eat in. It's a good mental exercise to ask yourself 'why would my audience share this with their friends?', and it's a much better question to ask than 'how can we go viral?'

The serious stuff

People soon started to see the incredible power social media has not just to connect friends and family but also the role it plays in major events. News gets broken, politicians debate and people let their family members know they are safe from a disaster – all on social media. It's the natural evolution of communications that people use social media for all aspects of their lives rather than just the fun things.

It's important to understand this, as often social media is treated by organizations as just a marketing tool, or for light-hearted content. A worrying number of organizations that deal with large-scale events do not consider how they will play out on social media. If you're considering a career in social media, you'll be very appealing to potential employers if you can demonstrate you are cool in a crisis. Obviously, some of these scenarios are major ones in which you may not have any involvement. But if you want to seek a career in journalism, government or even large charities, it becomes a lot more likely. And any organization should be mindful of what events are currently playing out nationally to prevent any inappropriate content being published.

So what sort of events could you potentially be dealing with if you are managing a professional social media account?

Disaster response

It's a part of modern life that natural disasters or those caused by humans will play out on social media too. People at the scene will be sharing content, broadcasting live and potentially adding to any hysteria. Commentary from news organizations around the world will quickly start appearing, while government agencies and law enforcement issue updates through social media.

You may need to filter this information quickly for many organizations – you could be a journalist trying to establish what's happening, working for a disaster relief charity to find people in need, or working for the government. It's important to act quickly and accurately – two things that often don't work well together. Most social networks allow you to filter by location and the type of profile. Avoid any that have just been set up or have anonymous profiles – sadly, hoaxers always try to trick people in these situations.

It's important to use social media to issue important information and updates in these situations as it will often be people's first port of call when they hear an event has occurred. People may be sharing content that's inappropriate and may need reporting. You can also ask people to share the imagery they have captured, as this benefits both reporters and government alike.

If, as is most likely, your organization has no link to events (for example, if you work for a product marketing company), you'll need to quickly review your current campaigns and check that nothing is inappropriate. Putting everything on pause will probably be a step too far, but check everything over to prevent a PR disaster.

Civic engagement

Social media is being used more and more by government and politicians. Certainly Donald Trump's election in 2016 had a lot to do with Twitter, although this may not be the best example to use.

Despite the prevalence of social media, it's a sad fact that many politicians are yet to realize its importance. There are challenges – you'll read about echo chambers shortly. But social media helps remind people they need to register to vote, take part in referenda or surveys, and campaign for the causes they care about. While people rarely convince those with different opinions by arguing with them on the internet, social media at its best should allow them to engage positively with their elected representatives and improve their civic lives.

If you work in any public sector communications role, civic engagement will be an important part of it.

Crisis communications

You never know when a crisis could hit your organization. It could be a PR fiasco, a controversy engulfing a senior member of staff, or a disastrous product launch. While you may never know if it's going to happen, you absolutely want to be as prepared as you can be when it does. You can't just go silent – social media abhors a vacuum. But how do you respond to a flood of angry social media posts? How do you keep your team calm and focused? Practising crisis response is absolutely essential. You can find really good simulators that aren't online but simulate a pretend social media storm. It is a good idea to get your team doing these fairly regularly as well as having a clear and practised crisis plan in place.

Trolling

Sad but true – at some point internet trolls are likely to appear. Trolls are people posting inflammatory, hateful or personal comments, often anonymously, to cause upset and mischief. It's unpleasant at the very least and can be extremely disheartening if you've put lots of effort into your content. It can also make it hard to get people unsure of social media to use it if they are nervous about getting trolled.

Actively moderate the comments, put filters in place in advance and use the traffic light community moderation system to judge what is and isn't appropriate. Fundamentally, you should never be nervous about deleting comments or banning someone. People may complain about their freedom of speech, but that doesn't apply to your channels in particular – you set the rules, so don't let people make you feel bad about enforcing them.

Tone of voice

The importance of tone of voice has been mentioned a few times throughout this book and it's just as vital to an effective social media brand. The brand's tone of voice is just as important as your visual style and subject matter.

When it comes to social media, this doesn't just mean writing your posts in a certain way. It informs how you interact with people, how you manage live broadcasts on social media, and the subjects you choose to cover. If you're commissioning a video or graphic design, you'll need to think about the language used within it too, so it fits into your social media tone of voice.

Generally speaking, social media is a very relaxed but intimate way of communicating. People won't expect stuffy language and, with attention at a premium, you need to be concise yet compelling. This goes against the grain for a lot of organizations, especially those used to dealing in formal language. It's a lot harder for legal firms or engineering companies to adapt their usual manner of communicating.

In the earlier section in Chapter 2 on creating a style guide, you read about creating a document people can refer to. By combining this with the traffic light moderation system, you can really enhance your social media brand's tone of voice in a safe way. It will help your team decide which people to respond to and what style of language you should use. Too often large organizations stick to very formal, dry language that simply isn't interesting. So tone-of-voice guidance should also govern when (and when not) to be light-hearted, make jokes or use emojis.

If your organization interacts with the public in any way, it's very likely your social media channels will become one of the main ways people review your organization and complain about it. Deleting any complaints or negative comments would be a very bad idea – even if it is very tempting. It would immediately create a backlash and exacerbate the problem. Think about how you or your team would handle these complaints and what language you would use. It's important to be empathetic, understanding and clear. You can incorporate this into your traffic light guidance too.

Having a clear and unique tone of voice can really help your channels stand out in the social media noise, especially if people know they can interact with you in an entertaining way. Brands like Innocent Drinks and Wendy's have been using this to great effect. It's easier said than done, though – getting a team of people to all have one unique, entertaining voice is difficult. It will take a lot of practice and guidance for people to get right. Again, having a style guide to refer to will make it an awful lot easier. Having a language obsessive on your team certainly helps too – someone who isn't just a grammar pedant but really understands how different styles of writing and use of words will be perceived by people.

You should try to develop your tone-of-voice skills. This means not only developing your own unique tone of voice but also learning to adapt to different styles. If you worked for a digital agency you'd be managing lots of different social media accounts for very different customers. You could switch from a youth-focused sports brand to a legal firm. By developing these skills you can demonstrate to your potential employers that you can easily start producing content for them in their house style.

Challenges

Echo chambers

Social networks are designed to help us connect to people, events and subjects we find most interesting. At first, this was presented as a utopian vision where people could learn and discover more than ever before. But as a system designed to show people things they are interested in based largely on algorithms, the opposite has in fact happened. People create their own digital worlds, largely showing them the things they like, the opinions they agree with and the products they already use. This problem has been called an echo chamber (or sometimes a filter bubble). While many argue about problems of fake news or inappropriate content on social media, this problem is often overlooked. It's especially prevalent during elections or referenda – people will very rarely see content from opposing viewpoints. We can all be guilty of it in small ways. When a friend has a child, it usually doesn't take me long to unfollow them if they just post endless photos of their baby. We create feeds for ourselves perfectly calibrated to show us only the things we want.

This has enormous problems for society as a whole and more specifically for any publishers of content. It means that while you may be able to speak effectively to an audience that's broadly supportive of what you do, it can be extremely hard to break into bubbles of people who are not aware of you or already supportive. As an example, let's take a government department or charity that gives foreign aid to needy countries. You may have a large, highly engaged audience of people who care deeply about supporting countries in times of hardship. But if you are given the brief to help convert sceptics of foreign aid to be supportive of your efforts, you will find it extremely hard to do so. Social media's algorithms are designed not to show this content to people who don't want to see it. There isn't an easy solution either, but some options include paid-for advertising or working with influencers popular with those audiences.

The move to messaging

It didn't take long for people to realize that broadcasting to the world on social media wasn't always a good idea. Teenagers found their parents trying to add them on Facebook, potential employers trawled people's Twitter feeds for potentially inappropriate content, and people became more aware of privacy issues.

Over time, more and more social media communication has been through the medium of messaging apps – Snapchat, released in 2011, is probably the most famous example of this. Networks based on private messaging, disappearing content and anonymous profiles have exploded in popularity.

These pose a challenge for the digital content producer. Rather than publishing content to a public, engaged audience, you may find they reside on private messaging apps. These can be hard to publish content through or capture any meaningful data about your audience. They have advantages, though – they provide an incredibly convenient way to broadcast to an audience quickly, gather opinion or user-generated content, or operate in countries with draconian surveillance laws. Thinking about how your content may be shared quickly through messaging apps is important, as is having a way for the people who use them to contact you.

Augmented reality

Augmented reality is usually discussed in terms best saved for science fiction. It's quite likely that, by the time you're reading this, you're not doing so through robotic eyeballs beaming content straight into your brain (I could be wrong). It's not science fiction, though – half a billion people have downloaded *Pokemon Go*. Augmented reality is most likely the next frontier of digital content as smart devices become better at interacting with the real world. This means the methods people use to consume content will become even more disparate, with the emphasis being on timely, useful information. It has huge opportunities for storytellers too – it's incredibly exciting to think how fiction and the real world could be blended. Think about getting people to travel through a set route, with interactive prompts along the way found using their smartphone, for example.

This is an exciting time for the opportunities offered by augmented reality, meaning that the challenge to you is a big one – people are still trying to figure out what works. But this challenge is also an opportunity. If you have an understanding of augmented reality and ideas about how a brand could use it, you'll have a competitive edge when looking for roles.

Common mistakes

Trying to be everywhere

Unless you have a huge team and a big budget, it's certain you won't be able to be on every social media network effectively. And you probably don't need to be. A lot of organizations feel that they have to be on a number of different social networks just for the sake of it. You're much better off strategically choosing one or two networks and really focusing on them rather than causing a lot of stress by being on too many, with poor-quality content being posted to each one.

Broadcasting rather than having a conversation

It's too easy just to post stuff to your social media channels and think the job's finished. If you never speak to your audience, you'll never learn what is and isn't working. More importantly, people expect to be able to interact with their favourite publishers, so if you only broadcast, your audience will get bored very quickly.

No strategy

Without a proper social media strategy, why are you even doing it? Publishing content to social media just for the sake of it is a waste of everyone's time. You won't know how to measure success, what your team is working towards, and how you'll identify important new networks. Sadly, too many publishers think just sending stuff out to social media means the job is done.

Thinking social media is facile

It isn't.

Exercise

This exercise is designed for people who are on social media, and those who are yet to join.

If you already use social media

If you're already on a particular network (it doesn't matter which one), think about one or two of the brands, people or organizations you follow and enjoy seeing content from. This exercise is designed to get you thinking about what it is about them you enjoy and being more analytical in your approach to social media.

Look back at their posts and complete Table 7.1.

Table 7.1 Social media analysis

What do they do well?
What range of content do they have?
What content don't you like and why?
How do they respond to negative comments?
How is their tone of voice consistent over time?

If you don't use social media

If you don't already use social media, let's get you started. It's important to stress you don't have to set up a profile in your own name if you feel nervous. Instead, you can simply create a pretend company and experiment with publishing posts until you feel more confident.

Use the previous section about how to choose the right channel. Think about what you want your pretend company to be and what audience it would want to reach. Then go ahead and set up a profile on that channel. If you're unsure about which network is right for the audience, don't worry – some simple online research should give you the answers as it's a topic many organizations publish about.

Once you're up and running, you can put the skills learnt from the rest of this book to good use.

Summary

Now we've covered the principles of social media in some detail, we'll move on to perhaps the hardest part of all – humans. You can learn how to produce great video or plan a brilliant campaign. If you're working with other people, it won't amount to much if they're not on board with it all too.

People

08

- Changing an organization's culture is essential if it doesn't embrace digital.
- Building a network of supporters will make your life a lot easier.
- Too many focus just on the technology or platform – culture and content are just as important.

Despite all the plans you make or creative ideas you come up with, your success will very much depend on people: your colleagues or collaborators, your audience, your customers. Digital is something that is still 'happening' and changing rapidly. This book has made the point a number of times that people are often fearful of digital. But what they are actually scared of is large-scale change – something that has always made people nervy. Digital can be seen by many as something that might put their jobs at risk or change what skills they need.

If you follow a career in digital content you'll likely encounter this. You may work in a traditional PR agency that knows how to hammer the phones to journalists or launch an event, but the staff don't understand social media. You may work in a newsroom where seasoned print reporters fear that digital storytelling signals the end of their career. Or you could work in a business where negative customer reviews online are ignored and nimble competitors are thriving. Influencing these people and getting them to support, or at the very least acknowledge, your efforts will be a crucial factor in how successful you are.

It's not all about other people either. The digital world does move quickly and it can sometimes feel like it's hard to keep up. You have to take risks and immediately discover if they have been successful or not. Over time, you can easily find yourself becoming more cautious. If you become too risk-averse, your content and channels will quickly become stale, with your audience leaving you as a result.

Changing people's perceptions can be extremely difficult, as can any sort of organizational change. With digital, however, you do have some advantages. There is overwhelming evidence that it's a vital part of any modern communication, data to back up your arguments and an active digital community to speak with.

There are often structural problems, though. You may come into an organization with a remit to improve their digital content, but discover you're part of the technology team rather than editorial or communications. At media organizations that involve another format (a print magazine or a TV channel, for example), you may find they don't work with the digital team or share their material. The overall structure of the organization may make it difficult to share digital skills and knowledge with people. You could even all be in different locations and time zones, for example.

The good news is that all these problems can be solved. Organizational or cultural change is nearly always a big part of being successful in digital content. While this can be hard, don't let it dissuade you. It's difficult, but that also makes it rewarding to get right. And you can't do anything new in your professional life if you don't take people with you.

What might some of the people you work with be like?

Types of people you'll encounter

In my career I've found people tend to fall into a few categories when it comes to digital content. Perhaps these are true for any profession, but there are a few challenges that are peculiar to content.

Ambassadors

If only everyone could be like the ambassadors. They are the people in your organization who just get it. They understand the importance of digital, support what you're trying to do, and are good at sharing their knowledge and enthusiasm with others.

They will be absolutely crucial to your success. If you work in a smaller organization, you can act as the main 'go-to' person for all the digital work. But medium to large organizations mean you simply can't be everywhere at once. People also tend to listen more to those from their own teams.

Therefore building and nurturing a network of in-house digital ambassadors, formally or informally, will help you build support for your digital strategy.

If you are charged with promoting an organization with digital content, you'll also need to know what's going on. By building an internal network of 'reporters' you can help keep informed about interesting stories within the organization. With the prevalence of smartphones, your ambassadors can capture and share content too.

Host regular catch-ups with your ambassador network and, most importantly, listen to their ideas. They will provide a near limitless supply of creative ideas and inspiration.

Sceptics

The sceptics are the opposite of ambassadors. These are the people who don't support what you're doing and may actually seek to disrupt it. Despite the temptation, they shouldn't be classed as the bad guys. They can actually help you, especially if they become converts (more on them shortly).

The reasons for their opposition may be many and complex, but often come down to two themes – tradition and fear. Because digital content is very different from other forms of communication, it can sometimes be hard for those with a background in traditional platforms to accept the role of digital. 'We've always done it this way' is a terrible reason to do anything. If you want to produce a video, saying we've always made them five minutes long and widescreen because that works on telly isn't the answer for social media.

Underneath this cynicism is sometimes the same worry discussed earlier, that digital may be a career threat. While it's important for any communicator to embrace digital content, it doesn't mean all other platforms or formats will disappear.

There are also those who simply think that digital doesn't matter or that it's facile. These are often the hardest people to convince.

If you come up against cynics, you have to be clear and confident. Explain simply why digital content is important to the organization, back your arguments up with data and use your ambassadors to help you make the case. It may take time to win them over, so persevere. When your content starts succeeding, it will be harder for people to disagree. While you need to be firm with cynics, it's also important not to come across as arrogant or as a know-it-all. You have to listen and address their concerns.

Ideally you'll win over as many of the cynics as you can. Some of them are likely to go further and become converts.

Converts

When you win sceptics over they can sometimes become converts – who, like ambassadors, champion digital content and support your strategy. They are arguably more effective than ambassadors in convincing people of the value of digital content because they have changed from a position of opposition to support. They are excellent at helping you convince sceptics and they act as influencers throughout the organization.

The power of having supporting 'converts' is why it's important not to be dismissive or too aggressive towards sceptics. If you alienate them, you may be missing out on the opportunity to have some of your most influential supporters.

'Experts'

Social media in particular is one of those subjects that many people who use it think they are experts in. People working in the digital world may often hear things like 'My nephew is on Snapchat, why aren't we using that?' or 'Why aren't we making video like these guys?'

This can be hard to deal with. Once you've produced a digital strategy that's right for your organization, you may find lots of people pitching in thinking they know best. It can feel as if your strategy is being undermined or make you doubt what you're doing.

It would be very misguided to think one person has all the answers. Naturally, sharing ideas with others, seeking challenge or opinion, and discussion are absolutely vital to success. The difference here is when people who don't have real knowledge or whose roles have nothing to with your organization's digital content try to unhelpfully derail or alter effective strategies.

A proper digital content strategy will be backed up by research and insight into your target audiences. Use this to help dissuade people who are trying to meddle. Ultimately it's a question of confidence. At this point you will have your role in digital content for a reason. That doesn't mean you have all the answers, but it's your speciality and that carries weight. Don't let people grind you down.

There's another kind of expert to watch out for – the digital one. Another result of the prevalence of digital communications is the increasing number of digital specialists. Of course, most of them are professional and can be extremely useful if your organization needs to bring in more digital support. But there are also quite simply a lot of charlatans out there. You can usually spot these people by their overwhelming use of digital gobbledegook, a reliance on vanity metrics or a lack of transparent data about their work. Any digital experts you bring in should be able to explain their work clearly, should be set clear SMART objectives and should share any metrics they can provide about their work.

Learning to embrace the risks of digital

Risk is a word that comes up a lot now. It's also a bit of a dirty word. Taking risks is seen as intrinsically scary or to be minimized at all costs. Not only would life be extremely boring if we never took risks, but never taking them is guaranteeing failure. Organizations and the people within them have to take risks whether they like it or not. Taking risks is how you keep your digital content fresh and exciting, find new opportunities for your organization and make continuous improvement the basis of all your team does.

Perhaps risk taking is something that doesn't come naturally to you. It's certainly easier to suggest than to actually do. It's natural to worry about what will happen if something goes wrong or what your colleagues may think. Risk taking is something you can get into the habit of, though. Start really small and often. You'll soon learn that disaster doesn't strike. You can then build up to bigger things.

Whoever leads a team has an obvious impact on it. If you can lead by example and show how important being flexible and innovative is, your team will follow too.

Digital content isn't really that risky. If you produce some poor-quality content, you may offend the audience but it's unlikely to be any worse than that. But given you're communicating with the public, it can feel more intimidating than it needs to be. It would be naive to think that digital PR disasters don't have potentially catastrophic effects on brands or organizations. These situations tend to be very rare, and the risk reduces as your team or organization increases their digital skills and audience understanding.

You may be the reverse – you could be a highly confident, experienced creative who is used to being innovative. If this is the case, there's another cultural problem to watch out for – getting into a creative rut. Without realizing it, you can find yourself sticking to the same formats, the same content ideas and the same creative solutions without even realizing it. This problem can actually be made worse by digital analytics. Once you establish a few content formats that you know work well, it can be extremely hard to convince your team to try anything different. But audiences can be fickle, and you need to try new things to figure out what works.

To combat this, you can be quite hard-line about it and set a quota – say one in ten pieces of content needs to be radically different from what you normally produce. It's debatable whether you can force creativity, but this approach certainly keeps you on your toes. It's also worth allotting time specifically to research what other creatives are doing. Spending a little time each week looking for fresh inspiration and seeing what the competition is doing can be really worthwhile.

Reassuring your team that risk taking is not only encouraged but essential to success can be reinforced by rewarding those who do try something new. In Chapter 6 on evaluation, different ideas for rewarding people were listed. You should consider rewarding your team on innovation and initiative rather than outright success – for example someone who produced a really different, creative video that may not have been hugely successful in terms of views. The success here would be that they tried something new rather than always rewarding sheer numbers of views.

Digital content's place in the organization

In the first chapter of this book I wrote that virtually all organizations need to communicate on digital channels and therefore produce great content. If you get a role where you're responsible for producing content, you should consider how that fits into the wider organization. We've looked at cultural change, and part of succeeding at that is having a clear narrative about why the organization is investing in producing digital content. Ultimately you need to champion the work you and your team (if you have one) do to the wider organization.

Narrative

Think of your team's narrative as your 'elevator pitch'. If someone who works with you bumps into you in the lift and says 'I don't know why we bother making videos for social media', how will you convince them in 30 seconds?

Your team, like any other, will require resources that may be hotly contested, especially if it's a smaller organization with limited funding. It's important to justify why it's essential to invest in digital content. This is even more crucial if you are working in a largely sceptical organization (perhaps one that's just started 'going digital'). There will be plenty of people grumbling about digital, but you can help convince them with a clear 'sales pitch'.

The reasons may be simple market forces – your audience may largely communicate through digital channels, so it's important to be on them. Revenues from digital could be rapidly rising, which makes arguing that it's not important a lot harder (some may try, though). Your narrative can also cover the opportunities investing in digital content brings, not only for the organization but also for the specific people working there. By being successful you're creating exciting new roles for people and building up digital skills across the organization.

Your narrative can also act as a mission statement for your team, helping everyone to understand how your work benefits your audiences, customers and colleagues.

Team structure

Digital content teams can end up being put in some strange places in the organization. Often your work will be mistaken for something technology related, meaning you're placed in the technology or IT department. Given your main role is communicating, this is always a bad choice. In most organizations you should be situated wherever most of the communicating is done – be it a newsroom, marketing team, press team or production crew.

You could be located in your own separate team – this makes sense with very large organizations but for small to medium-sized teams it's usually a mistake. You'll have lots of freedom but you're also separated from the main organization. It can be hard to build up digital skills in other teams or influence what they are doing. For organizations of this size, especially those that have very varied audiences or channels, a distributed structure often works well. This is when you place your digital team throughout the organization. For example, in a news organization you could have digital content specialists in the print team, the website team, a social media team and on the editorial desk. In a charity you may have them in the fundraising team, with the marketing professionals and with the public engagement team. The advantage of this model is that digital content becomes 'business as usual' much faster and allows you to get a much better understanding of what's going on throughout the organization. The drawback is that if you're leading that digital team, it can be hard to coordinate and build a real sense of teamwork among your digital professionals.

Opportunities

Digital content provides you with virtually unlimited creative opportunity. While this book has covered the importance of recognizing that many people are nervous about digital, the reverse is also true. Many people are intrigued by it, and if you're leading your organization's digital efforts you may quickly discover people asking to find out more about what you do. Consider hosting mini-internships or secondments for other people in the organization. This is the perfect way to raise digital's profile in the organization as well as helping you spot potential talent. It also helps you build the ambassador network we covered in the earlier section on the types of people you'll encounter.

How to build a creative team culture

Working in digital content means that you are, on a fundamental level, a creative. Some people are naturally gifted with creativity, and anyone working in this field has to have some affinity for it. Despite this, it's important to build a culture of creativity if you manage a team, especially to avoid the sort of creative rut mentioned in the earlier section. Here are some ideas on how to keep your team creative and motivated.

Criticize very, very rarely (at first)

When your team or someone new to digital is starting out, it will naturally take time for them to get up to a professional standard. Their initial efforts may not be up to your expected standard and the temptation to meddle will be very strong. As hard as it is in these early stages, I firmly believe it's more important to build up their confidence than to get the content perfect at the expense of their morale. Be encouraging, offer feedback on how they can improve, but keep it positive and resist the urge to micromanage.

Creative away days

The words 'away day' often fill people's hearts with dread – but it doesn't have to be this way. Rather than contrived team-building exercises, give your team a day where they can tell a story they want to – no limits. Encourage them to produce a video or a photo series, or to write a piece about a subject they are passionate about. They can then share their efforts at the end of the day. This exercise is especially useful if, as a team, you tend to cover the same subjects repeatedly.

Work with other organizations

This may be a lot harder in the private sector where working with your competitors would be a bad idea. But where possible, it's really valuable to visit other organizations' digital teams and see how they do things. You can get real inspiration from these visits but also discover what challenges they face. If competition isn't an issue, you could even give each other one of your projects to work on and see how a different team with a totally fresh pair of eyes handles the challenge.

Tell a totally different story

Similar to the creative challenge you can set your team members, why not get them to collectively tell a totally different story every now and again? It doesn't ever have to go public, but can be an excellent way of getting them to think differently. If they publish youth-focused music or comedy content, get them to try covering a serious news story (or vice versa). They will learn new storytelling methods and it will give them something fresh to try.

Developing your leadership skills

When you first lead a team, you will probably suffer from a large bout of imposter syndrome – feeling as if there's no way you can do this and that you don't know what you're doing. The bad news is this will probably not go away. The good news is everyone feels like it. Pretty much everyone has to lead at some point in their careers, and the first time you do it is just that – the first time. It's natural to feel nervous.

Working in digital content brings some other challenges that have already been mentioned – possible cultural problems, people being cynical about digital or thinking they know best. The results of your work are also being published to the public, who can give instant feedback – positive or otherwise.

Here are some principles of leadership that I believe are especially important when leading a creative digital content team.

Relax

This doesn't mean stop working hard. Creativity and confidence can often be fleeting things and are therefore hard to nurture. People you work with will pick up on whatever 'vibes' you are giving out. A nervous, risk-averse leader will make their entire team feel the same way and absolutely stifle their creativity. You will certainly feel anxious or unsure at times, but try to keep calm and project an image of confidence. However…

Listen

Don't mistake the previous advice for carte blanche to dictate everything or think you always need to have the answer. An effective creative leader is one who listens to their team. Frequently ask for their ideas or views, allow them to take the initiative when they need to, and foster (constructive) disagreement. Your team can provide you with a never-ending supply of great ideas, so you will miss out if you don't let them contribute.

Be clear

When you're presenting a new innovation, giving guidance or training staff, be as clear and as concise as possible. Levels of digital understanding and skills can often be low, so jargon or buzzwords will confuse both your message and your audience.

Teams never thrive when they don't know what direction they are heading in. It also makes people uncertain if they don't know what their leader's priorities are. It's also natural for people to feel passionately about their creative work and they often react badly to criticism. But clear, understandable reasons for requesting change go down a lot better than vague feedback.

Use data

Data could be one of the most valuable commodities in the modern economy and can inform everything you do – leadership included. You can't rely on data alone (your presentations would become very boring indeed), but by backing up your plans, insights and arguments with data you have concrete evidence to point to. A mix of your instincts and data-backed learning will make you an extremely effective leader.

Share creative ideas

Share the new, creative ideas you and your team have with your organization and others. The digital community is a very active one and people love hearing about new ideas. If you do produce a really successful, new creative way of telling stories, people will probably rip it off anyway, so you might as well make sure your team gets the credit. This can also help you establish yourself within the industry and raise your profile.

Pet projects matter

Google famously gave its employees 20 per cent of their time to work on something that interested them separate from their usual work. They have now abandoned this, but that doesn't mean the principle is not still a good one. Similar to the importance of listening, your team needs to feel valued and motivated. Give them time to pursue projects or ideas that interest them when you can, and it's likely you'll be rewarded not only with happier colleagues but also with new and interesting ideas.

Networking tools

The popularity of messaging and social media has changed our professional lives too. Nobody likes being swamped with e-mails or meeting requests. New, more convenient ways of communicating have emerged. Slack, a messaging platform, was released in 2013 and quickly became popular. You can message colleagues instantly rather than drafting lengthy e-mails. In 2016, Facebook launched a

Workplace version of the social network. This allowed people to share what they are working on, message colleagues and share content.

These tools serve an important purpose beyond making communication easier. What is traditionally called internal communications is crucial in any medium-sized or large organization. If you're in a digital content role, you'll need to be aware of what's going on in order to find good story ideas or user-generated content you may be able to use. If you're part of a digital change programme, then communicating this clearly and inviting discussion will be a central part of this.

It also allows you to share your internal narrative – explain to colleagues why digital content is important to the organization, champion the great work your team is doing and share positive feedback from your customers, beneficiaries or stakeholders.

The tools can really benefit your content team by allowing fast conversation and easy file transfer – something that's easily overlooked but very useful.

These internal social networks or messaging platforms can really help your organization. There are a couple of common mistakes, though, that people can make when deciding to use them:

- *Thinking 'job done'.* Getting everyone to use a tool like Slack doesn't mean you've achieved any digital transformation. People will quickly stop using it if you don't keep championing the importance of digital content and push transformation in person. The best way to convince people is in person as much as possible. Don't let fancy apps or platforms distract you from working with people face to face.

- *Ignoring user need.* Say a trendy new app comes along that's totally free to the organization to deploy. It can often be tempting to rush it out and pat yourself on the back for being so innovative. But what is the actual need for it?

    Find out what apps or services your team or colleagues like. What services do they actually need? What will actually make their working lives easier? Let the actual user need guide your decisions rather than deploying new platforms or tools for fashion's sake.

CASE STUDY Nick Shaw, Head of Digital at the England and Wales Cricket Board

Nick Shaw is the Head of Digital at the England and Wales Cricket Board. He was previously the Head of NOW TV Sports and before that the Head of Digital at the Rugby Football Union. I spoke to him about digital's place in an organization, how you influence people, and his thoughts on starting out in the industry.

Digital used to be treated as an afterthought by a lot of organizations. When I started in a digital role, social media was already huge, but senior leaders would think I was joking when I said the organization should be on social media too. They saw it as a threat or a risk, but as it grew and grew in popularity social media became harder to ignore. Despite this, it was still very hard to influence change and it really required senior buy-in.

Another challenge I used to find is that digital can be perceived as a cost, rather than an investment. Organizations have to see it this way because the world is becoming more digital – that's the way communication is going – so if they try to ignore it they just have to do it later on and find it much harder.

Because digital platforms are now so fragmented, it can be very hard to influence busy senior people, so you have to be very concise and clear about the benefits of digital and what you want to achieve. Sometimes people can think digital is just something that happens, without seeing the work that goes into it. Recently, a senior leader walked past my desk with all my screens open during a match. He was really surprised by how much data I had available. So I sat him down and talked him through all the content and analytics we had during just one match. He said: 'We need to get the CEO to sit down and see this too.'

You have to have a strategy behind your digital efforts rather than just 'doing digital'. A lot of organizations make the mistake of just pushing stuff out without thinking about the strategic value of their output. You can use research and data to show how your audience uses digital platforms to back up your arguments – with shock tactics occasionally. Getting people to understand how your audience consumes content is vital. For example, our younger audiences don't necessarily want to watch a full sports match or have the time, but want short clips across a lot of different platforms, so we provide that. Put the customer front and centre in everything you do.

When I sat down for my interview with the ECB, I asked them if digital had buy-in from the senior leadership team. As they did, I took the role. There has to be a commitment at a senior level, ie your CEO or board, to support digital, otherwise it won't really get anywhere.

Change can take time. Patience is important and you shouldn't feel disheartened if you don't get the change you want right away. As I think about our long-term strategy, we want to move our digital team from being a 'service' function to a 'sovereign' function, which is a big shift. We want to get ahead and ask what is the strategy behind the output, how can we use digital to support our goals, and then plan the content and channels from that.

Because so many people use digital, you get a lot of people in organizations thinking they understand it or know how the organization should be using it. This is great because it means more people are aware of it, but also potentially very dangerous. The fictional example I always give is that there is no way I would go out and set up a coaching course. But because digital is everywhere, there's a feeling that it's fine just to go off and do it, which means your brand, approach and organization can become fragmented. So we have worked on internal education to raise understanding of what we want to achieve and the best way of doing things.

Often organizations will build something and then forget about it. Think about how you can build and enhance these products or projects instead of just moving on to the next thing. Don't be afraid to fail, to try things out, and then close or change them if they aren't working. People can often be worried about admitting something hasn't worked, but it's the only way you succeed. Be bold enough to say 'we started this, it didn't give us the return we wanted, so let's try something else'.

If you want to work in digital, I'd say the main skills you need are actually applicable to most jobs. You need to be really clear and concise about what you want to achieve and why. You need to completely understand your audience and base your strategic decisions around that – who is your audience and where are they? I'm a bit unusual as a Head of Digital as I don't profess to be the most technically gifted. I think this is an asset, though, as it lets me focus on the opportunities that technology can bring rather than the detail of how it works under the hood.

Ultimately digital isn't rocket science – it's all about common sense. It's asking over and over what the audience wants and layering on a bit of technical nous to succeed.

Exercise

By this stage in the book you should have practised your content production and evaluation skills. You can now put them to the test for someone else. This will give you the opportunity to try to solve fresh creative challenges while again bolstering your portfolio and experience, thus making you more employable.

Get in touch with a local charity or community group whose work you support. Ask if they need any help with their digital efforts. You can explain that you want to build up your skills in this area and by working with an organization like theirs, you can put your skills into practice. This also stops the offer sounding patronizing.

Offer to provide the following:

- a digital 'audit' covering how they are currently doing on social media, where the opportunities for improvement are and what channels they do or don't need to be using;

- a content strategy with ideas for formats and easy-to-produce pieces of content to help boost their profile;

- a concise evaluation of their existing and new efforts to measure how successful your advice is.

Small charities are often desperate for digital support, so by contacting a few it's very likely you'll find some that could use your support. You'll also have real, tangible experience to demonstrate to employers how you've used your digital skills in the real-world environment.

Summary

The people you work with are fundamental to your success. They can be fiendishly hard to convince but can also serve as your best ambassadors. When thinking about digital content, don't just focus on the material you produce – pay close attention to those making it too.

Conclusion

We've covered a lot of ground in this book. I sincerely hope it helps you develop a fun and creative career in digital content. If you do, you'll discover there's still so much more to learn. Having an appetite for learning new skills and a curiosity for discovering how things work will be your greatest asset.

Some complain that the digital world is a fast-moving one – but that's exactly what makes it so exciting. As long as you keep your mind open and keep learning new things, you'll thrive. It might feel uncomfortable at first, but you can actually build up a habit of changing things or learning something new, and it becomes easier. If it never does feel easier, don't worry – it's natural to be nervous about change. But it's change that keeps life interesting.

As I've said a few times in this book, it's so important to your success and those around you that you take and encourage risk. The only way you can guarantee failure in life is by never taking a risk at all. You have to experiment with new ways of telling stories or producing content. If you're lucky enough to find yourself mentoring others, develop this sense of innovation in everything they do.

Ultimately digital, like so many other things, is most effective when you keep things simple. Focus on what your audience is interested in and how best to tell them the stories they're interested in, and you'll succeed.

If you are enthusiastic about what you've learnt in this book and you'd like to take your development further, think about what area you'd like to specialize in. By now you hopefully have an idea of whether you'd rather be, say, a marketer or a journalist. Decide how you'd like to use your digital content skills and develop those areas of knowledge.

You may also want to learn more advanced content skills. You may find a particular area interests you more than others. I started out producing video as I enjoyed it so much, and found learning more advanced skills easy because of my passion for it. It's always worth trying to learn new tricks and techniques. Keep an eye on what other people are doing to stay inspired and see how others have produced digital content in different ways.

Finally, whenever I work with a new team, I hand out these stickers in the photo. I'll tell you what three of the words stand for – just do it. You can spend a lot of time worrying about whether something is the right approach, whether you can learn these skills, or thinking you couldn't ever make it in a career in digital content.

If you have these negative thoughts or a lack of self-belief, I can only say these four letters to you:

INDEX

CPSIA information can be obtained
at www.ICGtesting.com
Printed in the USA
BVOW05s0035110118
505039BV00011B/51/P